AEROFILMS GUIDE

FOOTBALL GROUNDS

THIRTEENTH REVISED EDITION

AEROFILMS GUIDE

FOOTBALL GROUNDS

THIRTEENTH REVISED EDITION

Ian Allan
PUBLISHING

CONTENTS

CONTENTS

Front cover: **Work on the expansion at Norwich City's Carrow Road ground has seen the capacity increased to more than 26,000. Unfortunately, for the Canaries, this significantly increased capacity will grace the League Championship in 2005/06 with the team having been relegated at the end of 2004/05.**

Preceding pages: **The winds of change are evident in north London as the new Emirates Stadium, home of Arsenal from the start of the 2006/07 season, approaches completion in the foreground with the club's current home, Highbury, in the background. Another north London project destined for completion in the near future is Wembley, although it appears, at the time of writing, that completion for the 2005/06 FA Cup final to be hosted there may not be achieved. If that's the case, the FA Cup will return to the Millennium Stadium in May 2006.**

First published in 1993;
Reprinted 1993 (twice); Second edition 1994; Third edition 1995; Fourth edition 1996; Fifth edition 1997; Sixth edition 1998; Seventh edition 1999; Eighth edition 2000; Ninth edition 2001; tenth edition 2002; 11th edition 2003, reprinted 2003. 12th edition 2004; 13th edition 2005.

ISBN 0 7110 3056 1

Published by Ian Allan Publishing
an imprint of Ian Allan Publishing Ltd, Hersham, Surrey KT12 4RG.
Printed in England by Ian Allan Printing Ltd, Hersham, Surrey KT12 4RG

Code: 0508/G2

Text © Ian Allan Publishing Ltd 1993-2005
Diagrams © Ian Allan Publishing Ltd 2000-5
Aerial Photography © Simmons Aerofilms

Simmons Aerofilms Limited have been specialists in aerial photography since 1919. Their library of aerial photographs, both new and old, is in excess of 1.5 million images. Aerofilms undertake to commission oblique and vertical survey aerial photography, which is processed and printed in their specialised photographic laboratory. Digital photomaps are prepared using precision scanners.

Free photostatic proofs are available on request for any site held within the collection and price lists will be forwarded detailing the size of photographic enlargement available without any obligation to purchase.

Introduction

Welcome to the 13th edition of *Aerofilms Guide: Football Grounds*. As in previous years, the book has been fully revised to take account of the changes that have occurred to the grounds of the 92 members of the Football and Premier leagues.

In terms of new grounds, there are only two clubs — Coventry City and Swansea City — that will be starting the new season at new homes. Both of these new grounds look impressive and your editor looks forward to sampling their delights during the new season. Elsewhere, a number of clubs, most notably Arsenal at Highbury, are due to move imminently and, if you haven't as yet had the opportunity to visit this ground as well as those at Shrewsbury, Milton Keynes and elsewhere that are on the 'hit-list', the 2005/06 season may well be your last opportunity. Whilst the improved facilities that the new grounds offer are always welcome it is a shame when traditional grounds, with their history, disappear. Both Highbury and the Gay Meadow have a long history; whilst significant parts of Highbury are listed and will feature in any future redevelopment, the Gay Meadow, as with so many other grounds is largely unprotected but it has a character all of its own. Whilst the coracle in the Severn may be no more, its location close to the centre of one of England's most historic towns is attractive. In 12 months time, however, if all goes according to plan, the old ground will be no more to be replaced with some new residential development and whilst the new ground may be safe from flooding it will lack the character of the old. Such is progress!

Apart from the two new grounds, the 2005/06 season also welcomes back two old league clubs — Barnet and Carlisle United — from the ranks of the Nationwide Conference and, again if work is completed, the FA Cup Final will return to London and the rebuilt Wembley Stadium. Again, the new stadium looks impressive and will no doubt be a superb venue for the Cup Final and international matches in the future even though it lacks, at present, the history and traditions of the twin towers.

As this introduction is penned, the pre-season friendlies are about to start. This is the time of year when all fans, irrespective of club, can look forward to the new season with expectation. Some will have their expectations fulfilled, others will end up disappointed. Whatever your team, we hope that you will find this book of use and will have an enjoyable and successful 2005/06 season.

Aerofilms

Aerofilms was founded in 1919 and has specialised in the acquisition of aerial photography within the United Kingdom throughout its history. The company has a record of being innovative in the uses and applications of aerial photography.

Photographs looking at the environment in perspective are called oblique aerial photographs. These are taken with Hasselblad cameras by professional photographers experienced in the difficult conditions encountered in aerial work.

Photographs taken straight down at the landscape are termed vertical aerial photographs. These photographs are obtained using Leica survey cameras, the products from which are normally used in the making of maps.

Aerofilms has a unique library of oblique and vertical photographs in excess of one and a half million in number covering the United Kingdom. This library of photographs dates from 1919 to the present day and is being continually updated.

Oblique and vertical photography can be taken to customers' specification by Aerofilms' professional photographers.

To discover more of the wealth of past or present photographs held in the library at Aerofilms or to commission new aerial photographs, please contact:

Simmons Aerofilms, 32-34 Station Close, Potters Bar, Herts EN6 1TL.
Telephone: 01707 648390   Fax: 01707 648399
Web-site: www.simmonsaerofilms.com   E-mail: info@aerofilms.com

Disabled Facilities

We endeavour to list the facilities for disabled spectators at each ground. Readers will appreciate that these facilities can vary in number and quality and that, for most clubs, pre-booking is essential. Some clubs also have dedicated parking for disabled spectators; this again should be pre-booked if available.

MILLENNIUM STADIUM

Westgate Street, Cardiff CF10 1JA

Tel No: 0870 013 8600
Fax: 029 2023 2678
Stadium Tours: 029 208 22228
Web Site: www.millenniumstadium.com
E-Mail: info@cardiff-stadium.co.uk
Brief History: The stadium, built upon the site of the much-loved and historic Cardiff Arms Park, was opened in 2000 and cost in excess of £100 million (a tiny sum in comparison with the current forecast spend of over £600 million on the redevelopment of Wembley). As the national stadium for Wales, the ground will be primarily used in sporting terms by Rugby Union, but will be used by the FA to host major fixtures (such as FA Cup and Carling Cup finals) until, in theory, 2006 when the new Wembley is scheduled for completion.
(Total) Current Capacity: 72,500
Nearest Railway Station: Cardiff Central
Parking (Car): Street parking only.
Parking (Coach/Bus): As directed by the police
Police Force and Tel No: South Wales (029 2022 2111)
Disabled Visitors' Facilities:
Wheelchairs: c250 designated seats. The whole stadium has been designed for ease of disabled access with lifts, etc.
Blind: Commentary available.
Anticipated Development(s): None planned

KEY
Office address:
Millennium Stadium plc,
First Floor, Golate House,
101 St Mary Street,
Cardiff CF10 1GE

⬆ North direction (approx)

❶ Cardiff Central station
❷ Bus station
❸ River Taff
❹ Castle Street
❺ Westgate Street
❻ Wood Street
❼ Tudor Street
❽ High Street
❾ St Mary Street
❿ To Cardiff Queen Street station

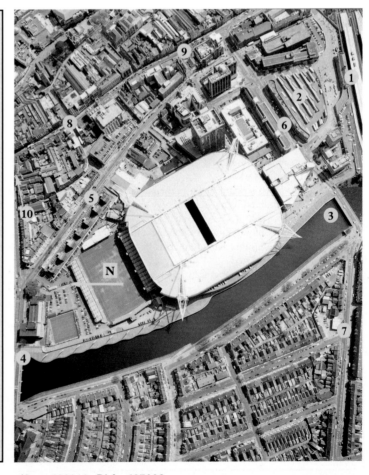

Above: 688019; Right: 687998

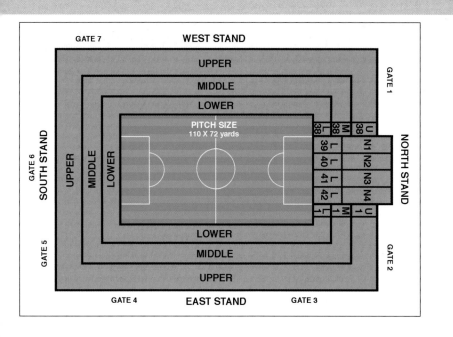

GATE 7

WEST STAND

UPPER

MIDDLE

LOWER

PITCH SIZE
110 X 72 yards

GATE 1

GATE 6

SOUTH STAND

UPPER | MIDDLE | LOWER

L 38 | M 38 | U 38

L 39 | N1

L 40 | N2

L 41 | N3

L 42 | N4

L 1 | M 1 | U 1

NORTH STAND

GATE 2

LOWER

MIDDLE

UPPER

GATE 5

GATE 4

EAST STAND

GATE 3

ARSENAL

Arsenal Stadium, Avenell Road, Highbury, London, N5 1BU

Tel No: 020 7704 4000
Advance Tickets Tel No: 020 7704 4040
Fax: 020 7704 4001
Web Site: www.arsenal.com
E-Mail: info@arsenal.co.uk
League: F.A. Premier
Brief History: Founded 1886 as Royal Arsenal, changed to Woolwich Arsenal in 1891, and Arsenal in 1914. Former grounds: Plumstead Common, Sportsman Ground, Manor Ground (twice), moved to Arsenal Stadium (Highbury) in 1913. Record attendance 73,295
(Total) Current Capacity: 38,548 (all seated)
Visiting Supporters' Allocation: 2,644 (maximum; all seated Clock End and Lower Tier West Stand)
Club Colours: Redcurrant, white shorts (commemorative for last season at Highbury)

Nearest Railway Station: Drayton Park or Finsbury Park (main line). Arsenal (tube)
Parking (Car): Street Parking
Parking (Coach/Bus): Drayton Park
Police Force and Tel No: Metropolitan (020 7263 9090)
Disabled Visitors' Facilities:
  Wheelchairs: Lower tier East Stand
  Blind: Commentary available
Anticipated Development(s): The club is moving forward with the development of the new 60,000-seat £350 million stadium at Ashburton Grove and plans to start the 2006/07 season at the new ground. Once the team moves from Highbury the existing ground will be redeveloped, although this work will incorporate the listed East and West stands.

KEY

C Club Offices
S Club Shop
E Entrance(s) for visiting supporters

⬆ North direction (approx)

❶ Avenell Road
❷ Highbury Hill
❸ Gillespie Road
❹ To Drayton Park BR Station (¼ mile)
❺ Arsenal Tube Station
❻ Clock End
❼ St Thomas's Road (to Finsbury Park station)
❽ North Bank
❾ West Stand
❿ East Stand

Above: 688318; *Right:* 688311

Following the 2003/04 season, where the Gunners had triumphed in the Premier League without being defeated, there were two big questions for Arsene Wenger's team to face in 2004/05: could the club retain the championship in the face of Chelsea's relentless spending spree and could the squad make a serious challenge for the Champions League? The Premier League was again a three-horse race, but in 2004/05 Chelsea were to prove dominant with Arsenal finishing second 12 points adrift and the Champions League also proved to be a disappointment. In terms of silverware, the Gunners had to be satisfied with the FA Cup, where the team made history in defeating Manchester United at the Millennium Stadium — it was the first occasion on which the cup had been won on a penalty shoot-out with the actual match ending 0-0 after extra time. This season marks Arsenal's final campaign at Highbury before the move to the new Emirates Stadium in 2006/07. To mark the occasion, the club has reverted to the original strip used when it first played at Highbury in 1913. During 2004/05 a number of young players came to the fore in the team and, with the experience they gained during the season they should be ideally placed once again to compete once again for the Premier League title and for the other domestic trophies.

ASTON VILLA

Villa Park, Trinity Road, Birmingham, B6 6HE

Tel No: 0121 327 2299
Advance Tickets Tel No: 0121 327 5353
Fax: 0121 322 2107
Web Site: www.avfc.premiumtv.co.uk
E-Mail: commercial.dept@astonvilla-fc.co.uk
League: F.A. Premier
Brief History: Founded in 1874. Founder Members Football League (1888). Former Grounds: Aston Park and Lower Aston Grounds and Perry Barr, moved to Villa Park (a development of the Lower Aston Grounds) in 1897. Record attendance 76,588
(Total) Current Capacity: 42,584 (all seated)
Visiting Supporters' Allocation: Approx 2,983 in North Stand
Club Colours: Claret and blue shirts, white shorts

Nearest Railway Station: Witton
Parking (Car): Asda car park, Aston Hall Road
Parking (Coach/Bus): Asda car park, Aston Hall Road (special coach park for visiting supporters situated in Witton Lane)
Police Force and Tel No: West Midlands (0121 322 6010)
Disabled Visitors' Facilities:
Wheelchairs: Trinity Road Stand section
Blind: Commentary by arrangement
Anticipated Development(s): In order to increase the ground's capacity to 51,000 Planning Permission has been obtained to extend the North Stand with two corner in-fills. There is, however, no confirmed timescale for the work to be completed.

KEY
- **C** Club Offices
- **S** Club Shop
- **E** Entrance(s) for visiting supporters
- **R** Refreshment bars for visiting supporters
- **T** Toilets for visiting supporters

↑ North direction (approx)

❶ B4137 Witton Lane
❷ B4140 Witton Road
❸ Trinity Road
❹ To A4040 Aston Lane to A34 Walsall Road
❺ To Aston Expressway & M6
❻ Holte End
❼ Visitors' Car Park
❽ Witton railway station
❾ North Stand
❿ Trinity Road Stand

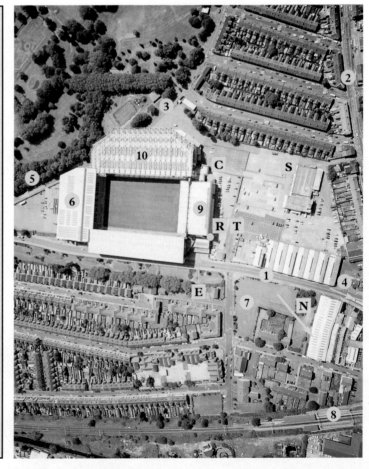

Above: 697435; Right: 697425

A hugely disappointing season for David O'Leary's team saw Villa ultimately finish in 10th position in the Premier League and lose to lower division teams in both of the domestic cup competitions: 3-1 away at Burnley in the third round of the Carling Cup and 3-1 away at Sheffield United in the third round of the FA Cup. In the Premier League, having ended 2003/04 on the verge of European football, perhaps the most disappointing aspect of the season for the Villa Park faithful was that the club made no serious challenge even for a UEFA Cup place in 2004/05. For 2005/06 much will depend upon O'Leary's activities in the transfer market. It has been suggested that the club may well be one of the more active participants in the market during the close season and this is essential if they are to acquire the players to mount a serious challenge during the new season. Failure to impress in the first months of the new campaign could see significant changes at Villa Park but it's hard to escape the conclusion that Villa may well struggle to better 10th place in 2005/06.

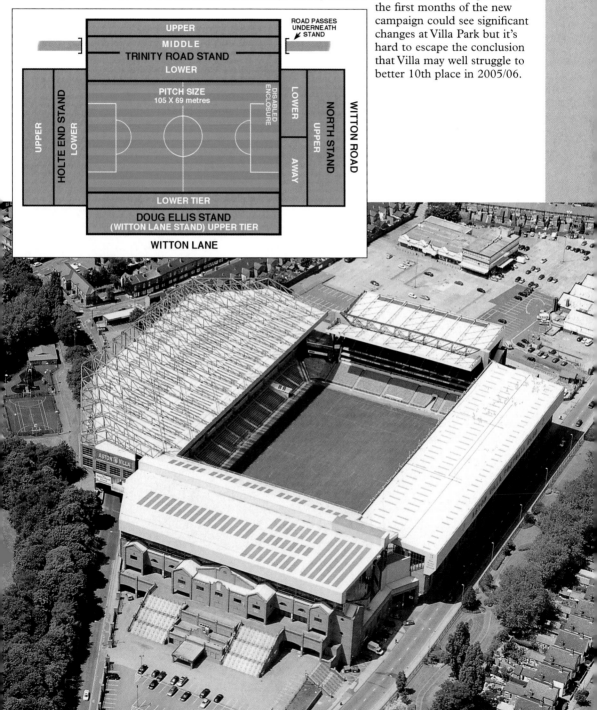

BARNET

Underhill Stadium, Barnet Lane, Barnet, Herts EN5 2DN

Telephone: 020 8441 6932
Advance Tickets Tel No: 020 8449 6325
Fax: 020 8447 0655
Web site: www.barnetfc.premiumtv.co.uk
E-mail: info@barnetfc.com
League: League Two
Brief History: Founded 1888 as Barnet Alston.
  Changed name to Barnet (1919). Former
  grounds: Queens Road and Totteridge Lane;
  moved to Underhill in 1906. Promoted to
  Football League 1991; relegated to
  Conference 2001; promoted to League 2
  2005. Record attendance, 11,026
(Total) Current Capacity: 4,057
Visiting Supporters' Allocation: 450 on East
  Terrace (nil seated)

Colours: Black and gold shirts, black shorts
Nearest Railway Station: New Barnet (High
  Barnet — Tube)
Parking (Car): Street Parking and High Barnet
  station
Parking (Coach/Bus): As directed by police
Police Force and Tel No: Metropolitan (020
  8200 2112)
Disabled Visitors' Facilities:
  Wheelchairs: 12 positions on east side of
  North Terrace
  Blind: No special facility
Anticipated Development(s):

KEY

C Club Offices
S Club Shop
E Entrance(s) for visiting
supporters
R Refreshment bars for visiting
supporters
T Toilets for visiting supporters

⬆ North direction (approx)

❶ Barnet Lane
❷ Westcombe Drive
❸ A1000 Barnet Hill
❹ New Barnet BR station
  (one mile)
❺ To High Barnet tube station,
  M1 and M25

Above: 699356; Right: 699359

After four seasons in the Conference, the Football League welcomes back Barnet. As with Chester in 2003/04, the 2004/05 campaign in the Conference was dominated by one team — Barnet — and it was not a question of whether the Bees won the title but the margin by which Paul Fairclough's team took the title in his first full season in charge. In the event, Barnet took the title comfortably, with a 12 point margin over second place Hereford United. With a squad full of both experience and youth, Fairclough will be hoping that his promoted team will emulate Yeovil, and challenge for promotion, rather than Chester, battling against relegation, in the challenge represented by League Two. In reality, the majority of fans would probably accept consolidation in League Two in 2005/06 with a view to providing the foundations for a push towards promotion at the end of 2006/07.

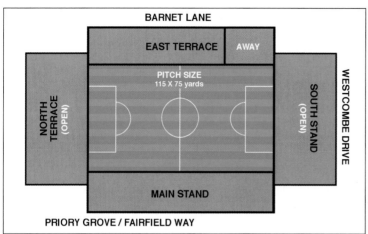

BARNSLEY

Oakwell Stadium, Grove Street, Barnsley, S71 1ET

Tel No: 01226 211211
Advance Tickets Tel No: 01226 211211
Fax: 01226 211444
Web Site: www.barnsleyfc.premiumtv.co.uk
E-mail: nickj@barnsleyfc.co.uk
League: League One
Brief History: Founded in 1887 as Barnsley St
Peter's, changed name to Barnsley in 1897.
Former Ground: Doncaster Road, Worsboro
Bridge until 1888. Record attendance 40,255
(Total) Current Capacity: 23,186 (all seated)
Visiting Supporters' Allocation: 6,000
maximum (all seated; North Stand)
Club Colours: Red shirts, white shorts
Nearest Railway Station: Barnsley

Parking (Car): Queen's Ground car park
Parking (Coach/Bus): Queen's Ground car
park
Police Force and Tel No: South Yorkshire
(01266 206161)
Disabled Visitors' Facilities:
  Wheelchairs: Purpose built disabled stand
  Blind: Commentary available
Future Development(s): With the completion
of the new North Stand with its 6,000
capacity, the next phase for the redevelopment
of Oakwell will feature the old West Stand with
its remaining open seating. There is, however,
no timescale for this work.

KEY

C Club Offices
S Club Shop
E Entrance(s) for visiting
supporters

↑ North direction (approx)

❶ A628 Pontefract Road
❷ To Barnsley Exchange BR
station and M1 Junction 37
(two miles)
❸ Queen's Ground Car Park
❹ North Stand
❺ Grove Street
❻ To Town Centre

14

Above: 697496; Right: 697497

Early March, following a run in which the team had won only two out of 13 games, saw Paul Hart leave Oakwell by mutual consent. He was replaced as caretaker-manager by Andy Ritchie. Under Ritchie the squad's performances improved immeasurably, with the team losing only twice in the last 11 games and with Ritchie winning Manager of the Month for March. With the season over, it was confirmed that Ritchie would the new permanent manager. Having secured Barnsley's League One status, finishing 13th was far better than might have been expected earlier, Ritchie has laid the foundations for perhaps better things in 2005/06 and fans will be hoping for a push towards the Play-Offs at the very least.

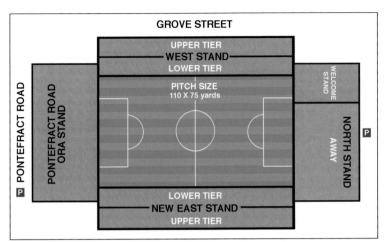

BIRMINGHAM CITY

St Andrew's Stadium, St Andrew's Street, Birmingham, B9 4NH

Tel No: 0871 226 1875
Advance Tickets Tel No: 0871 226 1875
Fax: 0871 226 1975
Web Site: www.bcfc.premiumtv.co.uk
E-Mail: reception@bcfc.com
League: FA Premier
Brief History: Founded 1875, as Small Heath Alliance. Changed to Small Heath in 1888, Birmingham in 1905, Birmingham City in 1945. Former Grounds: Arthur Street, Ladypool Road, Muntz Street, moved to St Andrew's in 1906. Record attendance 68,844.
(Total) Current Capacity: 30,016 (all seated)
Visiting Supporters' Allocation: 3-4,500 in new Railway End (Lower Tier)
Club Colours: Blue shirts, white shorts
Nearest Railway Station: Birmingham New Street
Parking (Car): Street parking

Parking (Coach/Bus): Coventry Road
Police Force and Tel No: West Midlands (0121 772 1169)
Disabled Visitors' Facilities:
  Wheelchairs: 90 places; advanced notice required
  Blind: Commentary available
Future Development(s): There are long term plans, in conjunction with the City Council, for the possible construction of a new 60,000-seat stadium to be shared with Warwickshire CCC at Digbeth. However, this is still at a very tentative stage and the club, in the short to medium term, has plans to expand St Andrews with the next phase of the redevelopment of the ground being the rebuilding of the Main Stand, possibly in 2007, taking the ground's capacity to some 36,500, but these will not be progressed if the Digbeth scheme goes ahead.

KEY

C Club Offices
S Club Shop
E Entrance(s) for visiting supporters

↑ North direction (approx)

❶ Car Park
❷ B4128 Cattell Road
❸ Tilton Road
❹ Garrison Lane
❺ To A4540 & A38 (M)
❻ To City Centre and New Street BR Station (1½ miles)
❼ Railway End
❽ Tilton Road End
❾ Main Stand
❿ Kop Stand
⓫ Emmeline Street
⓬ Kingston Road
⓭ St Andrew's Street

Above: 699252; Right: 699246

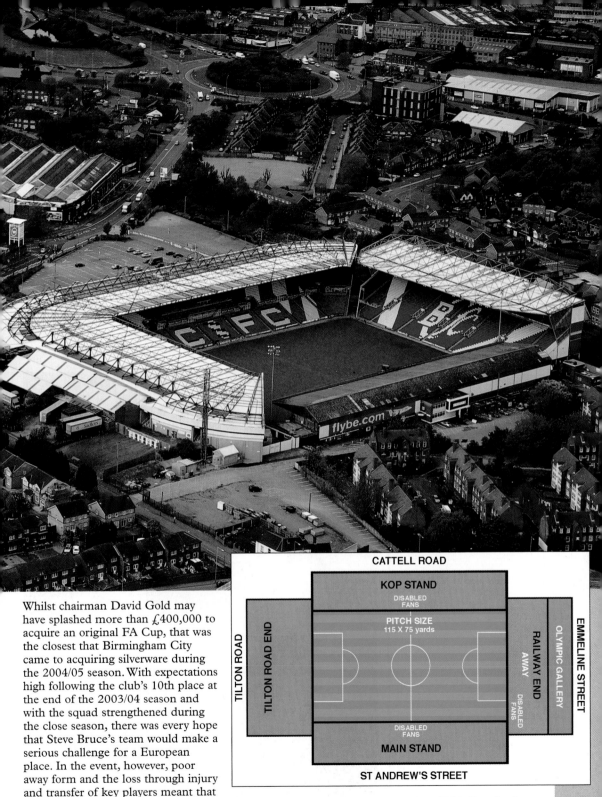

CATTELL ROAD

KOP STAND

DISABLED FANS

PITCH SIZE
115 X 75 yards

TILTON ROAD

TILTON ROAD END

RAILWAY END
AWAY

DISABLED FANS

OLYMPIC GALLERY

EMMELINE STREET

DISABLED FANS

MAIN STAND

ST ANDREW'S STREET

Whilst chairman David Gold may have splashed more than £400,000 to acquire an original FA Cup, that was the closest that Birmingham City came to acquiring silverware during the 2004/05 season. With expectations high following the club's 10th place at the end of the 2003/04 season and with the squad strengthened during the close season, there was every hope that Steve Bruce's team would make a serious challenge for a European place. In the event, however, poor away form and the loss through injury and transfer of key players meant that City were more likely to be dragged into the relegation mire than a place in the UEFA Cup. In the event the team finished in 12th position and for 2005/06 much will depend on how successful Bruce is in improving his squad. Now secure in the Premier League, City should have the potential to make a serious challenge for a European place and certainly improve on 12th position.

BLACKBURN ROVERS

Ewood Park, Blackburn, Lancashire, BB2 4JF

Tel No: 08701 113232
Advance Tickets Tel No: 08701 123456
Fax: 01254 671042
Web Site: www.rovers.premiumtv.co.uk
E-Mail: commercial@rovers.co.uk
League: FA Premier
Brief History: Founded 1875. Former Grounds: Oozebooth, Pleasington Cricket Ground, Alexandra Meadows. Moved to Ewood Park in 1890. Founder members of Football League (1888). Record attendance 61,783
(Total) Current Capacity: 31,367 (all seated)
Visiting Supporters' Allocation: 3,914 at the Darwen End
Club Colours: Blue and white halved shirts, white shorts
Nearest Railway Station: Blackburn

Parking (Car): Street parking and c800 spaces at ground
Parking (Coach/Bus): As directed by Police
Police Force and Tel No: Lancashire (01254 51212)
Disabled Visitors' Facilities:
  Wheelchairs: All sides of the ground
  Blind: Commentary available
Anticipated Development(s): There remain plans to redevelop the Riverside (Walker Steel) Stand to take Ewood Park's capacity to c40,000, but there is no confirmation as to if and when this work will be undertaken.

KEY
C	Club Offices
S	Club Shop
E	Entrance(s) for visiting supporters
R	Refreshment bars for visiting supporters
T	Toilets for visiting supporters

↑ North direction (approx)

❶ A666 Bolton Road
❷ Kidder Street
❸ Nuttall Street
❹ Town Centre & Blackburn Central BR station (1½ miles)
❺ To Darwen and Bolton
❻ Darwen End
❼ Car Parks
❽ Top O'Croft Road

Above: 698991; *Right:* 698999

The surprise appointment of Graeme Souness to the managerial role at Newcastle United left a vacancy at Ewood Park. With Tony Parkes stepping in briefly into his customary role of serial caretaker (for the last time as he left the club shortly afterwards), the club moved quickly to replace Souness with former striker Mark Hughes taking over in mid-September, having relinquished his role as manager of Wales. The new manager's task was to try and ensure Premier League survival, a feat that looked by no means certain for much of the campaign but which was ultimately achieved, along with an FA Cup semi-final against Arsenal. Under Hughes, Rovers acquired a reputation for robust play, encapsulated for many by the team's display in the game against Arsenal at the Millennium Stadium, but it proved

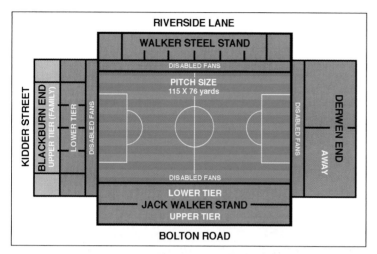

effective in dragging the team away from the drop zone. During the summer Hughes will undoubtedly be busy in the transfer market with rumours of departures and arrivals. The club should again secure Premier League status in 2005/06 but it's hard to escape the conclusion that a mid-table position is perhaps the best that the club can hope for.

BLACKPOOL

Bloomfield Road, Blackpool, Lancashire, FY1 6JJ

Tel No: 0870 443 1953
Advance Tickets Tel No: 0870 443 1953
Fax: 01253 405011
E-Mail: info@blackpoolfc.co.uk
Web Site: www.blackpoolfcpremiumtv.co.uk
League: League One
Brief History: Founded 1887, merged with 'South Shore' (1899). Former grounds: Raikes Hall (twice) and Athletic Grounds, Stanley Park, South Shore played at Cow Cap Lane, moved to Bloomfield Road in 1899. Record attendance 38,098
(Total) Current Capacity: 9,000 (all seated)
Visiting Supporters' Allocation: 1,700 (all seated) in East Stand (open)
Club Colours: Tangerine shirts, white shorts
Nearest Railway Station: Blackpool South

Parking (Car): At Ground and street parking (also behind West Stand – from M55)
Parking (Coach/Bus): Mecca car park (behind North End (also behind West Stand – from M55)
Other Club Sharing Ground: Blackpool Panthers RLFC
Police Force and Tel No: Lancashire (01253 293933)
Disabled Visitors' Facilities:
  Wheelchairs: North and West stands
  Blind: Commentary available (limited numbers)
Anticipated Development(s): The go-ahead has been given for the construction of a new £2 million South Stand. Once completed, this will add 2,000 seats to the ground's capacity although there is as yet no schedule for the work.

KEY

⬆ North direction (approx)

❶ Car Park
❷ To Blackpool South BR Station (1½ miles) and M55 Junction 4
❸ Bloomfield Road
❹ Central Drive
❺ Henry Street
❻ East Stand (away)
❼ Site of South Stand
❽ West (Pricebusters Matthews) Stand
❾ North Stand

Above: 699043; *Right:* 699048

Under tyro manager Colin Hendry it looked for the early part of the season as if Blackpool were in serious danger of losing their League One status, as the team resolutely failed to escape from the bottom four with just two points from their first seven games. However, the team's form improved after Christmas, with only one defeat between mid-January and mid-March, with the team gradually escaping from the drop zone. Finishing in 16th place on 57 points was better than might have been the case earlier and, with several promising players in his squad, Hendry will be optimistic of making significant progress in 2005/06. Providing that the team maintains its form from the second half of the 2004/05 season there is every possibility that the club will be able to make a challenge for the Play-Offs.

BLOOMFIELD ROAD

WEST STAND

PITCH SIZE
112 X 74 yards

P

NORTH STAND

EAST STAND (OPEN)
AWAY

BACK HENRY STREET

BOLTON WANDERERS

Reebok Stadium, Burnden Way, Lostock, Bolton, BL6 6JW

Tel No: 01204 673673
Advance Tickets Tel No: 0871 871 2932
Fax: 01204 673773
E-Mail: reception@bwfc.co.uk
Web Site: www.bwfc.premiumtv.co.uk
League: FA Premier
Brief History: Founded 1874 as Christ Church; name changed 1877. Former grounds: Several Fields, Pikes Lane (1880-95) and Burnden Park (1895-1997). Moved to Reebok Stadium for 1997/98 season. Record attendance (Burnden Park): 69,912. Record attendance of 28,353 at Reebok Stadium
(Total) Current Capacity: 28,723 (all-seater)
Visiting Supporters' Allocation: 5,200 maximum (South Stand)

Club Colours: White shirts, white shorts
Nearest Railway Station: Horwich Parkway
Parking (Car): 2,800 places at ground with up to 3,000 others in proximity
Parking (Coach/Bus): As directed
Police Force and Tel No: Greater Manchester (01204 522466)
Disabled Visitors' Facilities:
  Wheelchairs: c100 places around the ground
  Blind: Commentary available
Anticipated Developments(s): The station at Horwich Parkway has now opened. There are currently no further plans for the development of the Reebok Stadium.

KEY

⬆ North direction (approx)

❶ To Junction 6 of M61
❷ A6027 Horwich link road
❸ South Stand (away)
❹ North Stand
❺ Nat Lofthouse Stand
❻ West Stand
❼ M61 northbound to M6 and Preston (at J6)
❽ M61 southbound to Manchester (at J6)
❾ To Horwich and Bolton
❿ To Lostock Junction BR station
⓫ To Horwich Parkway station

Above: 699055; Right: 699053

A season of contrasts for Sam Allardyce's Bolton team saw considerable promise in the first few months of the campaign, followed by a dramatic slump in form that suggested that the team might get dragged towards the relegation dog-fight and then by a further reversal of form that saw the team threaten a place in the Champions League. Who needs a roller-coaster in Bolton when you've got Wanderers? In the event, a top-four finish was just beyond the team's capabilities, but in finishing sixth the team ensured that it would be playing in the UEFA Cup for the first time. It took several years, but Bolton would now appear to have consolidated its membership of the Premier League and another season with at least a top-half finish would seem to be the likely result in 2005/06. The only fly in the ointment

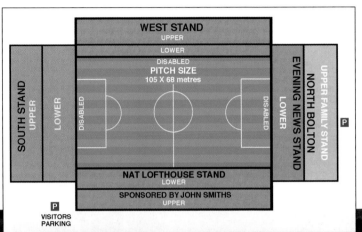

might be the distraction of European competition. In the past teams have reached Europe and have lost sight of the league — most notably Ipswich Town in recent seasons — and have ended up battling to avoid the drop. Allardyce is probably an astute enough manager to avoid this at the Reebok Stadium but adding additional games, with the threat of injuries, might pose a problem.

BOSTON UNITED

York Street, Boston, Lincolnshire PE21 6JN

Club Offices: 45 Wide Bargate, Boston, Lincolnshire PE21 6SH
Tel No: 01205 591900
Advance Tickets Tel No: 01205 364406
Fax: 01205 359153
Web Site: www.bostonunited.co.uk
E-mail: info@bostonunited.co.uk
League: League Two
Brief History: Boston Town was established in the 1880s and commenced playing at York Street. The club dropped the 'Town' suffix after World War 1 and re-formed as Boston United in 1934. The team won the Conference title in 1977 but was not allowed into the league due to the standard of the ground. The title was won again in 2002 and the club entered the Nationwide League at the start of the 2002/03 season. Record attendance 11,000
(Total) Current Capacity: 6,643 (1,769 seated)
Visiting Supporters' Allocation: 1,821 (no seated) in Town End Terrace

Club Colours: Amber and black hooped shirts, black shorts
Nearest Railway Station: Boston (one mile)
Parking (Car): Limited parking at the ground; recommended car park is the John Adams NCP
Parking (Coach/Bus): As directed
Police Force and Tel No: Lincolnshire (01205 366222)
Disabled Visitors Facilities:
  Wheelchairs: Finn Forest Stand
  Blind: No special facility
Future Development(s): The club has plans for the construction of a new 7,500-seat stadium in the Broadsides area of the town. The ground, anticipated to cost £8 million, will also provide a home for non-league Boston Town and is hoped to be available, subject to planning permission, by the start of the 2007/08 season. The work will be part funded by the sale of York Street and Tattershall Road (the home of Boston Town) for redevelopment.

KEY

E Entrance(s) for visiting supporters

R Refreshment bars for visiting supporters

T Toilets for visiting supporters

↑ North direction (approx)

❶ John Adams Way
❷ Spilsby Road
❸ Haven Bridge Road
❹ York Street
❺ Spayne Road
❻ River Witham
❼ Maud Foster Drain
❽ Market Place
❾ To bus and railway stations
❿ York Street Stand (away)
⓫ Spayne Road Terrace
⓬ Town End Terrace
⓭ Finnforest Stand

Above: 693105; Right: 693098

A season of consolidation for Steve Evans and his Boston side saw the Pilgrims finish the League Two season in 16th position some 14 points below the Play-Offs. However, whilst there was some progress at home, the club's away form wasn't great and the weakness of the defence negated the fact that the team was one of the division's top scorers. However, top scorer Andy Kirk was sold to Northampton and whether the Pilgrims can make progress in 2005/06 will depend on Evans' skill in replacing him. It's hard to escape the conclusion that a further season of mid-table mediocrity beckons at York Street.

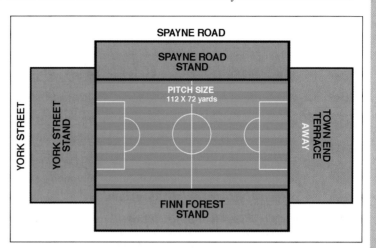

A.F.C. BOURNEMOUTH

The Fitness First Stadium at Dean Court, Bournemouth, Dorset, BH7 7AF

Tel No: 01202 726300
Advance Tickets Tel No: 0845 330 1000;
 01202 726303
Fax: 01202 726301
E-Mail: enquiries@afcb.co.uk
Web Site: www.afcb.premiumtv.co.uk
League: League One
Brief History: Founded 1890 as Boscombe St.
 John's, changed to Boscombe (1899),
 Bournemouth & Boscombe Athletic (1923) and
 A.F.C. Bournemouth (1971). Former grounds
 Kings Park (twice) and Castlemain Road,
 Pokesdown. Moved to Dean Court in 1910.
 Record attendance 28,799; since rebuilding:
 8,819
(Total) Current Capacity: 10,300 (all seated)
Visiting Supporters' Allocation: 1,500 in East
 Stand (can be increased to 2,000 if required)

Club Colours: Red and black shirts, black shorts
Nearest Railway Station: Bournemouth
Parking (Car): Large car park adjacent ground
Parking (Coach/Bus): Large car park adjacent
 ground
Police Force and Tel No: Dorset (01202 552099)
Disabled Visitors' Facilities:
 Wheelchairs: 100 spaces
 Blind: No special facility
Anticipated Development(s): In early July – after
 the cut-off for photography for this edition – it
 was announced that the club intended to
 construct a temporary stand at the south of the
 ground to provide accommodation for 1,100 for
 the start of the 2005/06 season, taking Dean
 Court's capacity to over 10,000.

KEY

C Club Offices

↑ North direction (approx)

❶ Car Park
❷ A338 Wessex Way
❸ To Bournemouth BR Station
 (1½ miles)
❹ To A31 & M27
❺ Thistlebarrow Road
❻ King's Park Drive
❼ Littledown Avenue
❽ North Stand
❾ Main Stand
❿ East Stand
⓫ Site of South Stand
 (Temporary

Above: 695760; *Right:* 695749

Ultimately a season of some disappointment for Sean O'Driscoll's team as the Cherries, who had been in the Play-Off zone for much of the season, failed at the last, seeing the all-important sixth place snatched from them in the final game of the season. Two teams were in the frame for sixth — Bournemouth and Hartlepool. Ironically, Hartlepool were the visitors at Dean Court and, provided that Bournemouth won, the Play-Off place would be destined for the South Coast. In the event, managerless Hartlepool achieved a 2-2 draw, thereby grabbing the Play-Off place. Ultimately Bournemouth's fate resulted from a bad run of injuries and from poor home form in the latter part of the season; provided these can be put behind the club in 2005/06 there is every chance that the team will again feature in the battle for the Play-Offs.

MAIN STAND

PITCH SIZE
112 X 74 yards

SOUTH STAND
(TEMPORARY)

NORTH STAND

THISTLEBARROW ROAD

AWAY

EAST STAND

BRADFORD CITY

Valley Parade, Bradford, BD8 7DY

Tel No: 01274 773355
Advance Tickets Tel No: 01274 770022
Fax: 01274 773356
Web Site: www.bradfordcityfc.premiumtv.co.uk
E-Mail: bradfordcityfc@compuserve.com
League: League One
Brief History: Founded 1903 (formerly Manningham Northern Union Rugby Club founded in 1876). Continued use of Valley Parade, joined 2nd Division on re-formation. Record attendance: 39,146
(Total) Current Capacity: 25,136 (all seated)
Visiting Supporters' Allocation: 1,842 (all seated) in TL Dallas stand plus seats in Midland Road Stand if required
Club Colours: Claret and amber shirts, white shorts

Nearest Railway Station: Bradford Forster Square
Parking (Car): Street parking and car parks
Parking (Coach/Bus): As directed by Police
Police Force and Tel No: West Yorkshire (01274 723422)
Disabled Visitors' Facilities:
  Wheelchairs: 110 places in Sunwin, CIBA and Carlsberg stands
  Blind: Commentary available
Anticipated Development(s): With work on the Main (Sunwin) Stand now completed, Valley Parade has a slightly imbalanced look. The club has proposals for the reconstruction of the Midland Road (Yorkshire First) Stand to take the ground's capacity to 30,000, although, given the club's current financial position, there is no time-scale.

KEY

C Club Offices
S Club Shop
E Entrance(s) for visiting supporters
R Refreshment bars for visiting supporters
T Toilets for visiting supporters

↑ North direction (approx)

❶ Midland Road
❷ Valley Parade
❸ A650 Manningham Lane
❹ To City Centre, Forster Square and Interchange BR Stations M606 & M62
❺ To Keighley
❻ Car Parks
❼ Sunwin Stand
❽ Midland (Yorkshire First) Stand
❾ TL Dallas Stand
❿ Carlsberg Stand

Above: 692550; *Right:* 692545

MIDLAND ROAD

YORKSHIRE FIRST STAND   AWAY

| A | B | C | D | E | F | G |

DISABLED FANS

PITCH SIZE
110 X 80 yards

DISABLED FANS

| F | E | D | C | B | A |

LOWER

| N | M | L | K | J | H | G | UPPER

SOUTH PARADE

THORNCLIFFE ROAD

CARLSBERG STAND

UPPER — LOWER

M L K J H G — F E D C B A

HOLYWELL ASH LANE

TL DALLAS STAND

LA LB LC LD LE — UF UG UH UJ UK

Following the trauma of the close season, when the club was within hours of going out of business, most fans of the Bantams would have been quite pleased at the start of the 2004/05 campaign to have a team to support. In the event, however, by the end of the season fans were disappointed in the team's failure to maintain a push towards at least the Play-Offs or automatic promotion, both of which seemed possible in late October when Colin Todd received the League One Manager of the Month award. In the event, however, poor form at Valley Parade meant that the good work done away from home was wasted and the team finished in mid-table. The poor league form was compounded in the three cup competitions with the team losing to lower division teams in all three. For 2005/06, Todd has the basis of a good squad; with judicious strengthening in the close season, there is every possibility that City could prosper in the new campaign and this time make a serious bid for the Play-offs at least.

BRENTFORD

Griffin Park, Braemar Road, Brentford, Middlesex, TW8 0NT

Tel No: 0870 900 9229
Advance Tickets Tel No: 0870 900 9229
Fax: 020 8568 9940
Web Site: www.brentfordfc.premiumtv.co.uk
E-Mail: enquiries@brentfordfc.co.uk
League: League One
Brief History: Founded 1889. Former Grounds: Clifden House Ground, Benn's Field (Little Ealing), Shotters Field, Cross Roads, Boston Park Cricket Ground, moved to Griffin Park in 1904. Founder-members Third Division (1920). Record attendance 38,678
(Total) Current Capacity: 12,763 (8,905 seated)
Visiting Supporters' Allocation: 2,200 on Ealing Road Terrace (open) and 600 seats in Block A of Braemar Road Stand
Club Colours: Red and white striped shirts, black shorts
Nearest Railway Station: Brentford, South Ealing (tube)

Parking (Car): Street parking (restricted)
Parking (Coach/Bus): Layton Road car park
Other Club Sharing Ground: London Broncos RLFC
Police Force and Tel No: Metropolitan (020 8577 1212)
Disabled Visitors' Facilities:
  Wheelchairs: Braemar Road
  Blind: Commentary available
Anticipated Development(s): Although the club's long-term intention is to relocate, in mid-December 2004 it was announced that the Football Foundation would grant the club £1,775,950 for work at Griffin Park, provided that plans were approved at a public meeting. Planned work includes modification of the New Road Stand and the provision of a roof over the Ealing Road Terrace. Although the original application was rejected by the planning authorities in December, following local consultation plans were approved in mid-April. The work will ultimately result in a capacity of 15,000 at Griffin Park.

KEY

C Club Offices
S Club Shop

↑ North direction (approx)

❶ Ealing Road
❷ Braemar Road
❸ Brook Road South
❹ To M4 (¼ mile) & South Ealing Tube Station (1 mile)
❺ Brentford BR Station
❻ To A315 High Street & Kew Bridge
❼ New Road
❽ Ealing Road Terrace (away)
❾ Brook Road Stand

Above: 695938; Right: 695940

NEW ROAD

NEW STAND

PITCH SIZE
110 X 73 yards

BROOK ROAD

BROOK ROAD STAND

COVERED TERRACE

SEATS

DISABLED
FANS

EALING ROAD

EALING ROAD
TERRACE

UNCOVERED TERRACE

AWAY

PADDOCK

BRAEMAR ROAD STAND

AWAY

BRAEMAR ROAD

As a result of the impressive form shown by the Bees under his stewardship, Martin Allen's team managed to survive in 2003/04 in League One and they took the impressive end of season form through to the new campaign with the result that, whilst never in the hunt for one of the automatic promotion places, the team were always in the pack chasing a Play-Off position. Finishing in fourth place meant a semi-final against Paul Sturrock's Sheffield Wednesday team but, unfortunately, a 1-0 defeat at Hillsborough allied to a 2-1 reverse at Griffin Park means that the Bees will again be playing in League One in 2005/06. Allen has, however, proved that he can get much out of his squad and the Bees should again be one of the pre-season favourites for the Play-Offs at least. Away from the League, the team were potential giantkillers in the FA Cup when they drew 2-2 at Southampton in the fifth round of the FA Cup. However, the team wasn't able to make home advantage pay in the replay with Southampton progressing to the sixth round.

BRIGHTON & HOVE ALBION

Withdean Stadium, Tongdean Lane, Brighton BN1 5JD

Tel No: 01273 695400
Fax: 01273 648179
Advance Ticket Tel No: 01273 776992
Web Site: www.seagulls.premiumtv.co.uk
E-Mail: seagulls@bhafc.co.uk
League: League Championship
Brief History: Founded 1900 as Brighton & Hove Rangers, changed to Brighton & Hove Albion 1902. Former grounds: Home Farm (Withdean), County Ground, Goldstone Ground (1902-1997), Priestfield Stadium (ground share with Gillingham) 1997-1999; moved to Withdean Stadium 1999. Founder members of the 3rd Division 1920. Record attendance (at Goldstone Ground): 36,747; at Withdean Stadium: 6,995.
(Total) Current Capacity: 7,053 (all seated)
Visiting Supporters' Allocation: 800 max on open North East Stand
Club Colours: Blue and white striped shirts, white shorts
Nearest Railway Station: Preston Park
Parking (Cars): Street parking in the immediate vicinity of the ground is residents' only. This will be strictly enforced and it is suggested that intending visitors should use parking facilities away from the ground and use the proposed park and ride bus services that will be provided.
Parking (Coach/Bus): As directed
Police Force and Tel No: Sussex (01273 778922)
Disabled Visitors' Facilities
  Wheelchairs: Facilities in both North and South stands
  Blind: No special facility
Anticipated Development(s): The ongoing saga of the construction of the new stadium at Falmer continues with the plans now in the hands of the Deputy Prime Minister, John Prescott. The club is hoping that its League Championship status will encourage the government to give the project the go-ahead, but in the meantime it is also hoping to undertake further work at the Withdean Stadium to increase capacity there by 1,966 in the short term and an extension of its lease until 2008. The new stadium is anticipated to cost £44 million and provide a 22,000 all-seated capacity eventually. In late May 2005 it was announced by the Office of the Deputy Prime Minister that the club would have a decision by 31 October 2005 at the latest following the resumption of the public inquiry on 1 February 2005.

KEY

Club Address:
  8th Floor, Tower Point,
  44 North Road, Brighton
  BN1 1YR
  Tel: 01273 695460
  Fax: 01273 648179

Shop Address:
  6 Queen's Road, Brighton

⬆ North direction (approx)

Note: All games at Withdean will be all-ticket with no cash admissions on the day.

❶ Withdean Stadium
❷ London-Brighton railway line
❸ To London Road (A23)
❹ Tongdean Lane
❺ Valley Drive
❻ To Brighton town centre and main railway station (1.75 miles)
❼ Tongdean Lane (with bridge under railway)
❽ South Stand
❾ A23 northwards to Crawley
❿ To Preston Park railway station
⓫ North Stand
⓬ North East Stand (away)

Above: 698692; *Right:* 698698

Promoted at the end of the 2003/04 season, the Seagulls were one of the pre-season favourites to make an immediate return to League One, but in Mark McGhee the club has a manager well-experienced at this level and, whilst always part of the relegation battle, the team managed to survive, although it was not until towards the last game of the season that safety was assured. Three teams — Gillingham, Crewe and Brighton — were all in the frame for the drop, with Brighton's goal difference being the worst of the three. Fortunately for fans of the Seagulls, McGhee's team secured a valuable 1-1 home draw against high-flying Ipswich, the point being sufficient to lift the side into 20th place, one point off the drop zone. For 2005/06, the club again looks as though it will be one of the teams battling against the drop particularly as the promoted teams look stronger this season. If McGhee can get the club to 21st again it will be a considerable triumph.

WITHDEAN STADIUM

SOUTH STAND
UNCOVERED

DISABLED FANS
PITCH SIZE
110 X 75 yards

ELWOOD AVENUE

HOSPITALITY BOXES

UNDEVELOPED

DISABLED

AWAY

NORTH STAND

BRISTOL CITY

Ashton Gate Stadium, Ashton Road, Bristol BS3 2EJ

Tel No: 0117 963 0630
Advance Tickets Tel No: 0870 112 1897
Fax: 0117 963 0700
Web Site: www.bcfc.premiumtv.co.uk
E-Mail: commercial@bcfc.co.uk
League: League One
Brief History: Founded 1894 as Bristol South End changed to Bristol City in 1897. Former Ground: St John's Lane, Bedminster, moved to Ashton Gate in 1904. Record attendance 43,335
(Total) Current Capacity: 15,000 during redevelopment (all seated)
Visiting Supporters' Allocation: 3,000 in Wedlock End (all seated; can be increased to 5,500 if necessary) (location during redevelopment to be confirmed)
Club Colours: Red shirts, white shorts
Nearest Railway Station: Bristol Temple Meads
Parking (Car): Street parking

Parking (Coach/Bus): Marsh Road
Police Force and Tel No: Avon/Somerset (0117 927 7777)
Disabled Visitors' Facilities:
    Wheelchairs: Limited
    Blind: Commentary available
Anticipated Development(s): The club announced in late February that it intended to redevelop the East (Wedlock) Stand with work commencing during the summer of 2005. The work will cost £7 million and should be completed for the start of the 2006/07 season. In early May it was announced that the club had been awarded a £800,000 grant to fund the work. Once work is completed, capacity at Ashton Gate will be increased to 2,000 to 21,000 with the Wedlock Stand providing accommodation for 5,200; however, whilst work is in progress the ground's capacity will be reduced to 15,000.

KEY

C Club Offices
S Club Shop

↑ North direction (approx)

❶ A370 Ashton Road
❷ A3209 Winterstoke Road
❸ To Temple Meads Station (1½ miles
❹ To City Centre, A4, M32 & M4
❺ Database Wedlock Stand (prior to redevelopment)
❻ Atyeo Stand
❼ Brunel Ford Williams Stand
❽ Dolman

Above: 699164; Right: 699177

For tyro player-manager Brian Tinnion, the 2004/05 season — his first in charge — was ultimately one of disappointment for Bristol City as the club just failed to make the Play-Offs despite a last day victory at Sheffield Wednesday. Finishing seventh, one point below Hartlepool in the all-important sixth position, was probably a reflection of City's relative poor home form, as the club only achieved nine victories at Ashton Gate in the League during the season. In Leroy Lita City possessed one of League One's top scorers and, with his departure, there is every possibility that City may struggle in the battle for either automatic promotion or the Play-Offs. Off the field, Tinnion is hoping to strengthen the training squad with an experienced coach.

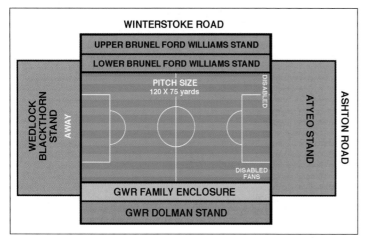

WINTERSTOKE ROAD

UPPER BRUNEL FORD WILLIAMS STAND

LOWER BRUNEL FORD WILLIAMS STAND

PITCH SIZE
120 X 75 yards

DISABLED

DISABLED FANS

WEDLOCK BLACKTHORN STAND

AWAY

ATYEO STAND

ASHTON ROAD

GWR FAMILY ENCLOSURE

GWR DOLMAN STAND

BRISTOL ROVERS

The Memorial Stadium, Filton Avenue, Horfield, Bristol BS7 0BF

Tel No: 0117 909 6648
Advance Tickets Tel No: 0117 909 6648
Fax: 0117 908 5530
Web Site: www.bristolrovers.premiumtv.co.uk
E-Mail: club@bristolrovers.co.uk
League: League Two
Brief History: Founded 1883 as Black Arabs, changed to Eastville Rovers (1884), Bristol Eastville Rovers (1896) and Bristol Rovers (1897). Former grounds: Purdown, Three Acres, The Downs (Horfield), Ridgeway, Bristol Stadium (Eastville), Twerton Park (1986-96), moved to The Memorial Ground 1996. Record attendance: (Eastville) 38,472, (Twerton Park) 9,813, (Memorial Ground) 9,274
(Total) Current Capacity: 11,917 (4,000 seated); standing capacity of 8,000 includes 500 on the Family Terrace
Visiting Supporters' Allocation: 1,132 (Centenary Stand Terrace; open)

Club Colours: Blue and white quartered shirts, white shorts
Nearest Railway Station: Filton or Stapleton Road
Parking (Car): Limited parking at ground for home fans only; street parking also available
Parking (Coach/Bus): As directed
Police Force and Tel No: Avon/Somerset (0117 927 7777)
Other Clubs Sharing Ground: Bristol Shoguns RUFC
Disabled Visitors' Facilities:
Wheelchairs: 35 wheelchair positions
Blind: Limited provision
Anticipated Development(s): Planning permission, with restrictions, was granted by the council in early June for the redevelopment of the Blackthorn End. This work, for which there is no reported timescale at present, will add a further 1,279 seats to the ground's existing capacity taking the total to some 13,000.

KEY

C Rugby Club offices
E Entrance(s) for visiting supporters
R Refrshments for visiting supporters
T Toilets for visiting supporters

↑ North direction (approx)

❶ Filton Avenue
❷ Gloucester Road
❸ Muller Road
❹ To Bristol city centre (2.5 miles) and BR Temple Meads station (3 miles)
❺ Downer Road
❻ Car Park
❼ To M32 J2 (1.5 miles)
❽ Strathmore Road
❾ To Filton (1.5 miles)
❿ Hill House Hammond Stand
⓫ West (Das) Stand
⓬ Blackthorn End
⓭ South Stand

Above: 699175; *Right:* 699180

Ultimately a disappointing season for Rovers and for manager Ian Atkins. Although the team finished in 12th position, a slight improvement on the 15th achieved the previous year, this result masked the fact that this was based upon a late improvement in form. Earlier in the campaign, whilst the team was never dragged into the battle to avoid the drop, fans would have been disappointed to see the team floundering in League Two's lower levels. Rovers undoubtedly has the potential to do better and, in Ian Atkins, a manager well experienced at this level. If the team can maintain the sort of form that it showed in the latter part of the season, then it should be competing for the Play-Offs; if not, then another season of mid-table mediocrity beckons.

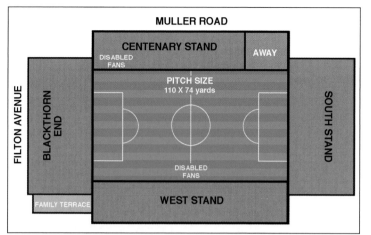

MULLER ROAD

CENTENARY STAND

DISABLED FANS

AWAY

PITCH SIZE
110 X 74 yards

FILTON AVENUE

BLACKTHORN END

SOUTH STAND

DISABLED FANS

FAMILY TERRACE

WEST STAND

BURNLEY

Turf Moor, Harry Potts Way, Burnley, Lancs, BB10 4BX

Tel No: 0870 443 1882
Advance Tickets Tel No: 0870 443 1914
Fax: 01282 700014
Web Site: www.burnleyfootballclub.premium.co.uk
E-Mail: m.greenhalgh@burnleyfc.com
League: League Championship
Brief History: Founded 1882, Burnley Rovers
(Rugby Club) combined with another Rugby
Club, changed to soccer and name to Burnley.
Moved from Calder Vale to Turf Moor in 1882.
Founder-members Football League (1888).
Record attendance 54,775
(Total) Current Capacity: 22,546 (all seated)
Visiting Supporters' Allocation: 4,125 (all
seated in David Fishwick [Cricket Field]
Stand)
Club Colours: Claret and blue shirts, white
shorts

Nearest Railway Station: Burnley Central
Parking (Car): Church Street and Fulledge
Rec. (car parks)
Parking (Coach/Bus): As directed by Police
Police Force and Tel No: Lancashire (01282
425001)
Disabled Visitors' Facilities:
Wheelchairs: Places available in North, East
and Cricket Field stands
Blind: Headsets provided with commentary
Anticipated Development(s): The club has
proposals for the redevelopment of the Cricket
Field (David Fishwick) Stand but this depends
on the relocation of the cricket club. The new
structure would provide seating for some
7,000. In the event of this option not proving
practical attention will turn to the expansion of
the Bob Lord Stand.

KEY

C Club Offices
S Club Shop
E Entrance(s) for visiting
supporters

⬆ North direction (approx)

❶ Brunshaw Road
❷ Belvedere Road
❸ Burnley Central BR Station
(1/2 mile)
❹ Cricket Ground
❺ Cricket Field Stand
❻ East (Jimmy McIlroy) Stand
❼ Bob Lord Stand
❽ North (James Hargreaves)
Stand

Above: 696988; *Right:* 696994

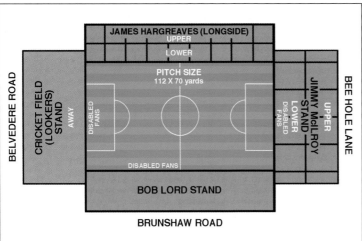

BELVEDERE ROAD

CRICKET FIELD (LOOKERS) STAND

AWAY

JAMES HARGREAVES (LONGSIDE)

UPPER

LOWER

PITCH SIZE
112 X 70 yards

DISABLED FANS

DISABLED FANS

BEE HOLE LANE

JIMMY McILROY STAND

UPPER

LOWER

DISABLED FANS

BOB LORD STAND

BRUNSHAW ROAD

Under Steve Cotterill for the first time, Burnley improved considerably on their 19th position in 2003/04 to end the season in 13th place. Apart from the better form in the league, the club also had the satisfaction of defeating Liverpool 1-0 at home in the third round of the FA Cup, the decisive strike being a bizarre own goal. In the fourth round Burnley were drawn against local rivals Blackburn Rovers; unfortunately, a draw at Turf Moor was followed by defeat at Ewood Park. In 2004/05 Cotterill laid the foundations of some solid progress but lack of resources may hamper the club if it is to progress much further. Potentially, in 2005/06, the club could be on the fringes of the Play-Offs, but perhaps a top half finish is the best that can be reasonably expected given the strength of the three relegated teams.

BURY

Gigg Lane, Bury, Lancashire, BL9 9HR

Tel No: 0161 764 4881
Advance Tickets Tel No: 0161 764 4881
Fax: 0161 764 5521
Web Site: www.buryfc.co.uk
E-Mail: info@buryfc.co.uk
League: League Two
Brief History: Founded 1885, no former names or former grounds. Record attendance 35,000
(Total) Current Capacity: 11,669 (all seated)
Visiting Supporters' Allocation: 2,676 (all seated) in West (Manchester Road) Stand
Club Colours: White shirts, royal blue shorts
Nearest Railway Station: Bury Interchange
Parking (Car): Street parking

Parking (Coach/Bus): As directed by Police
Police Force and Tel No: Greater Manchester (0161 872 5050)
Other clubcs sharing ground: FC United of Manchester
Disabled Visitors' Facilities:
  Wheelchairs: South Stand (home) and West Stand (away)
  Blind: Commentary available
Anticipated Development(s): The completion of the rebuilt Cemetery End means that current plans for the redevelopment of Gigg Lane have been completed.

KEY

C Club Offices

S Club Shop

E Entrance(s) for visiting supporters

↑ North direction (approx)

❶ Car Park
❷ Gigg Lane
❸ A56 Manchester Road
❹ Town Centre & Bury Interchange (Metrolink) (¾ mile)
❺ West (Manchester Road) Stand
❻ Cemetery End

Above: 696978; *Right:* 696984

GIGG LANE

MAIN STAND

MANCHESTER ROAD

WEST STAND
AWAY

PITCH SIZE
112 X 72 yards

DISABLED
FANS

DISABLED FANS

CEMETERY END
STAND

SOUTH STAND
MILLIKEN ENCLOSURE

One of a number of clubs troubled by financial problems during 2004/05, Bury unfortunately failed to capitalise on the success in reaching the Play-Offs in 2003/04 and slumped well down the League Two table in 2004/05, ultimately finishing in 17th place, as a result of severe pruning of the squad as manager Graham Barrow struggled against these financial problems. At one stage, moreover, it looked as though the team would be drawn into the relegation battle, although this was avoided. With the club now on a more secure financial basis, including the reacquisition of the freehold of Gigg Lane, Barrow can plan for 2005/06 with more confidence. Whilst the new season may be one of consolidation, the club has the potential to feature in the battle for the Play-Offs.

CARDIFF CITY

Ninian Park, Sloper Road, Cardiff, CF11 8SX

Tel No: 029 2022 1001
Advance Tickets Tel No: 0845 345 1400
Fax: 029 2034 1148
Web Site: www.cardiffcityfc.premiumtv.co.uk
E-mail: reception@cardiffcityfc.co.uk
League: League Championship
Brief History: Founded 1899. Former Grounds: Riverside Cricket Club, Roath, Sophia Gardens, Cardiff Arms Park and The Harlequins Rugby Ground, moved to Ninian Park in 1910. Ground record attendance 61,566 (Wales v. England, 1961)
(Total) Current Capacity: 20,000 (12,647 seated)
Visiting Supporters' Allocation: 2,000 maximum in John Smiths Grange End Terrace (limited seating)
Club Colours: Blue shirts, blue shorts

Nearest Railway Station: Ninian Park (adjacent) (Cardiff Central 1 mile)
Parking (Car): Opposite Ground, no street parking around ground
Parking (Coach/Bus): Leckwith Stadium car park
Police Force and Tel No: South Wales (029 2022 2111)
Disabled Visitors' Facilities:
Wheelchairs: Corner Canton Stand/Popular Bank (covered)
Blind: No special facility
Anticipated Development(s): In mid-December the plans for the new 30,000-seat stadium were hit when the council deferred a decision on the associated retail development until January.

KEY

C Club Offices
S Club Shop
E Entrance(s) for visiting supporters
R Refreshment bars for visiting supporters
T Toilets for visiting supporters (Terrace only, when used)

⬆ North direction (approx)

❶ Sloper Road
❷ B4267 Leckwith Road
❸ Car Park
❹ To A4232 & M4 Junction 33 (8 miles)
❺ Ninian Park Road
❻ To City Centre & Cardiff Central BR Station (1 mile)
❼ To A48 Western Avenue, A49M, and M4 Junction 32 and 29
❽ Ninian Park BR station

Above: 699068; *Right:* 699079

A disappointing season for City saw the team dragged in to the League Championship relegation battle as Lennie Lawrence fought to keep the Bluebirds up. Off the field, well reported financial problems threatened the club and led to the departure of many high-profile players, such as Robert Earnshaw to West Brom and Graham Kavanagh, as the desperate need to balance the club's books led to a fundamental weakening of the squad. Ultimately, the team finished in 16th position, four points off the drop zone, and at the end of May it was announced that Lawrence was standing down as manager (albeit with a consultancy role for at least six months). For 2005/06 much will depend on Lawrence's successor in the managerial hot seat, the experienced Dave Jones, and his ability with a much pared down team. It's hard to escape the conclusion that, with better resourced teams emerging from League One, the new season may well be a struggle to retain the club's League Championship status and a struggle that the team may ultimately lose.

CARLISLE UNITED

Brunton Park, Warwick Road, Carlisle, CA1 1LL

Telephone: 01228 526237
Advance Tickets Tel No: 01228 526327
Fax: 01228 530138
Web Site: www.carlisleunited.premiumtv.co.uk
E-mail: admin@carlisleunited.co.uk
League: League Two
Brief History: Founded 1904 as Carlisle United (previously named Shaddongate United). Former Grounds: Millholme Bank and Devonshire Park, moved to Brunton Park in 1909. Record attendance 27,500
(Total) Current Capacity: 16,651 (6,433 seated)
Visiting Supporters' Allocation: 1,700 (Petterill End Terrace — open — or north end of Main Stand)

Club Colours: Blue shirts, white shorts
Nearest Railway Station: Carlisle
Parking (Car): Rear of ground
Parking (Coach/Bus): St Aiden's Road car park
Police Force and Tel No: Cumbria (01228 528191)
Disabled Visitors' Facilities:
Wheelchairs: East Stand and Paddock (prior arrangement)
Blind: No special facilities
Anticipated Development(s):

KEY
C Club Offices
E Entrance(s) for visiting supporters
R Refreshment bars for visiting supporters
T Toilets for visiting supporters

↑ North direction (approx)

❶ A69 Warwick Road
❷ To M6 Junction 43
❸ Carlisle Citadel BR station (1 mile)
❹ Greystone Road
❺ Car Park
❻ Petterill End (away)

Above: 699882; Right: 699091

Welcome back to the Football League after one season out to Carlisle United. Following several years of battling against the drop, the Cumbrians finally succumbed to relegation at the end of 2003/04. Whilst the Nationwide Conference was dominated by Barnet, United was always in the hunt for the Play-Offs and Paul Simpson's side ultimately finished in third place, 13 points below promoted Barnet. In the Play-Offs, Carlisle faced Aldershot; a 1-0 defeat in Hampshire allied to a 2-1 victory at Brunton Park sent United into a penalty shoot out, in which the Cumbrians ultimately triumphed (despite going 3-1 down). Facing Stevenage in the final at Stoke, a 1-0 victory means that League football returns to the city. Over recent years, teams promoted through the Play-Offs from the Conference have had varied fortunes: Doncaster stormed to a second successive promotion but Shrewsbury Town struggled. Perhaps a season of consolidation is the best that the Brunton Park faithful can hope for.

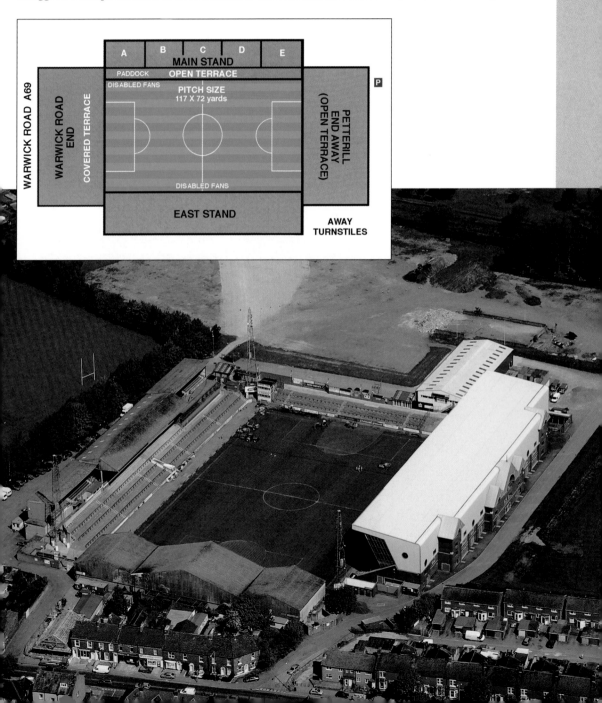

CHARLTON ATHLETIC

The Valley, Floyd Road, Charlton, London, SE7 8BL

Tel No: 020 8333 4000
Advance Tickets Tel No: 020 8333 4010
Fax: 020 8333 4001
Web Site: www.cafc.co.uk
E-Mail: info@cafc.co.uk
League: F.A. Premier
Brief History: Founded 1905. Former grounds: Siemens Meadows, Woolwich Common, Pound Park, Angerstein Athletic Ground, The Mount Catford, Selhurst Park (Crystal Palace FC), Boleyn Ground (West Ham United FC), The Valley (1912-23, 1924-85, 1992-date). Founder Members 3rd Division South. Record attendance 75,031
(Total) Current Capacity: 27,116 (all seated)
Visiting Supporters' Allocation: 3,000 (maximum; all seated in South Stand)

Club Colours: Red shirts, white shorts
Nearest Railway Station: Charlton
Parking (Car): Street parking
Parking (Coach/Bus): As directed by Police
Police Force and Tel No: Metropolitan (020 8853 8212)
Disabled Visitors' Facilities:
  Wheelchairs: East/West/South stands
  Blind: Commentary, 12 spaces
Anticipated Development(s): The club presented plans to Greenwich Council in mid-December for the redevelopment of the East Stand, taking the ground's capacity to 31,000. At the same time the club lodged outline plans for the redevelopment of the rest of the stadium with the intention of taking capacity to 40,600.

KEY

E Entrance(s) for visiting supporters

R Refreshment bars for visiting supporters

T Toilets for visiting supporters

↑ North Direction (approx)

❶ Harvey Gardens
❷ A206 Woolwich Road
❸ Valley Grove
❹ Floyd Road
❺ Charlton BR Station
❻ East Stand
❼ North Stand
❽ West stand
❾ South stand (away)
❿ Charlton Church Lane
⓫ Charlton Lane

Above: 699307; Right: 699295

Another season of ultimate disappoint for Alan Curbishley and Athletic saw the club once again threaten to achieve a European place, only for the campaign to fizzle out into a position of mid-table mediocrity. In 2003/04 Charlton finished in seventh position, just outside the UEFA Cup spots and in 2004/05 the club had the potential to do even better. Certainly, for the first part of the season, it looked as though the team would fulfil these expectations but, as in previous years, a late decline in form saw the team ultimately finish in 11th position and Curbishley start to question his own position.

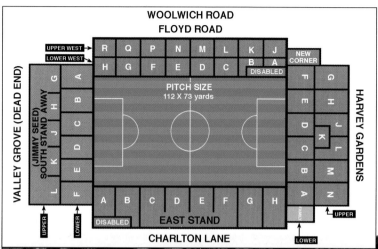

Now firmly established in the Premier League and capable of attracting big name signings, Athletic ought to be performing for a full season rather than only two-thirds. If they can sustain a full season, then a UEFA Cup spot should be achievable; if not, another season of mid-table anonymity beckons.

CHELSEA

Stamford Bridge, Fulham Road, London, SW6 1HS

Tel No: 0870 300 1212
Advance Tickets Tel No: 0870 300 2322
Fax: 020 7381 4831
E-Mail: No contact available for general inquiries via e-mail
Web Site: www.chelseafc.com
League: F.A. Premier
Brief History: Founded 1905. Admitted to Football League (2nd Division) on formation. Stamford Bridge venue for F.A. Cup Finals 1919-22. Record attendance 82,905
(Total) Current Capacity: 42,449 (all seated)
Visiting Supporters' Allocation: Approx. 1,600 (East Stand Lower; can be increased to 3,200 if required or 5,200 if part of the Matthew Harding Stand [lower tier] is allocated)

Club Colours: Blue shirts, blue shorts
Nearest Railway Station: Fulham Broadway or West Brompton
Parking (Car): Street parking and underground car park at ground
Parking (Coach/Bus): As directed by Police
Police Force and Tel No: Metropolitan (020 7385 1212)
Disabled Visitors' Facilities:
  Wheelchairs: East Stand
  Blind: No special facility
Anticipated Development(s): With the long awaited completion of the second tier of the West Stand now achieved, redevelopment of Stamford Bridge as a stadium is now complete.

KEY

⬆ North direction (approx)

❶ A308 Fulham Road
❷ Central London
❸ To Fulham Broadway Tube Station
❹ Mathew Harding Stand
❺ East Stand
❻ West Stand
❼ South (Shed) Stand
❽ West Brompton Station

Above: 697396; Right: 697393

The second year of the Roman occupation of Stamford Bridge saw Jose Mourinho's squad dominate the Premier League, taking the title well before the end of the season with a record number of points and victories. Increasingly, the Premier League is coming to be a three-horse race on an annual basis, with Manchester United and Arsenal representing the only real challenge to Chelsea domestically. The team will, occasionally, lose as they did to Newcastle United in the FA Cup, but in the Premier League, the Blues suffered only one defeat, at Manchester City, and only seven draws. The Championship wasn't Chelsea's only success during the year, as victory over Liverpool in the Carling Cup brought the first silverware of Mourinho's reign. However, not all was positive; failure for the second year running to get beyond the semi-finals of the Champions League, losing 1-0 to a contentious goal at Anfield against Liverpool, was disappointing, and to many outside the club Mourinho's intemperate comments and allegations of 'tapping up' potential players slightly tarnish the

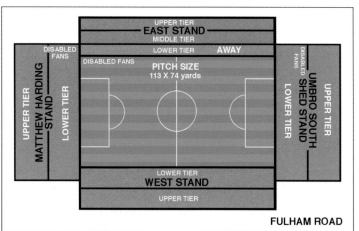

undoubted success that the club had had. It's hard to escape the conclusion that, with Arsenal in transition and Manchester United in some turmoil, the Premier League is Chelsea's again in 2005/06. However, the club will only be able to claim to have become one of the European greats if Abramovich's millions brings the Champions League trophy to Stamford Bridge.

CHELTENHAM TOWN

Whaddon Road, Cheltenham, Gloucestershire GL52 5NA

Tel No: 01242 573558
Advance Tickets Tel No: 01242 573558
Fax: 01242 224675
Web Site: www.cheltenhamtownfc.premiumtv.co.uk
E-Mail: info@ctfc.com
League: League Two
Brief History: Cheltenham Town was founded in 1892. It moved to Whaddon Road in 1932 having previously played at Carter's Field. After two seasons in the Conference it achieved Nationwide League status at the end of the 1998/99 season. Record attendance 8,326
(Total) Current Capacity: 7,407 (3,139 seated)
Visiting Supporters' Allocation: 2,100 (maximum) in Whaddon Road Terrace – uncovered – and in Wymans Road (In2Print) Stand
Club Colours: Red and white striped shirts, white shorts

Nearest Railway Station: Cheltenham (1.5 miles)
Parking (Car): Limited parking at ground; otherwise on-street
Parking (Coach/Bus): As directed by Police
Police Force and Tel No: Gloucestershire (01242 521321)
Disabled Visitors' Facilities:
  Wheelchairs: Six spaces in front of Main Stand
  Blind: No special facility
Anticipated Development(s): The long-awaited cover over the open Whaddon Road Terrace has, despite earlier forecasts, yet to be completed. Once this work has been undertaken the next phase in the development of the ground will be the rebuilding of the Main Stand, although there is no time-scale for this work.

KEY

C Club Offices
E Entrance(s) for visiting supporters

↑ North direction (approx)

❶ B4632 Prestbury Road
❷ Cromwell Road
❸ Whaddon Road
❹ Wymans Road
❺ To B4075 Priors Road
❻ To B4075 Prior Road
❼ To Cheltenham town centre and railway station (1.5 and 2 miles respectively)
❽ Main Stand
❾ Wymans Road Stand
❿ Prestbury Road End
⓫ Whaddon Road End

Above: 695569; Right: 695566

A disappointing season for Cheltenham saw the team finish, for the second season running, in 14th place. Under John Ward, the team had shown considerable progress towards the end of the 2003/04 season and, if that form had been replicated, then a Play-Off place was a distinct possibility. In the event, a poor start to the season, which saw the Robins secure only two wins in the first 11 matches, meant that the threat of relegation was a greater possibility than the promotion race. Things improved again in the later stages but, unless the team can sustain decent performances for a full season, a position of mid-table mediocrity again looks the likeliest result in 2005/06.

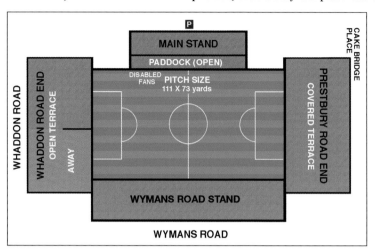

WHADDON ROAD

WHADDON ROAD END

OPEN TERRACE

AWAY

P

MAIN STAND

PADDOCK (OPEN)

DISABLED FANS

PITCH SIZE
111 X 73 yards

WYMANS ROAD STAND

WYMANS ROAD

CAKE BRIDGE PLACE

PRESTBURY ROAD END

COVERED TERRACE

CHESTER CITY

Saunders Honda Stadium, Bumpers Lane, Chester, CH1 4LT

Tel No: 01244 371376
Advance Tickets Tel No: 01244 371376
Fax: 01244 390265
Web-site: www.chestercityfc.net
E-mail: info@chestercityfc.net
League: League Two
Brief History: Founded 1884 from
amalgamation of Chester Wanderers and
Chester Rovers. Former Grounds: Faulkner
Street, Lightfoot Street, Whipcord Lane,
Sealand Road Moss Lane (Macclesfield Town
FC), moved to Deva Stadium 1992. Record
attendance (Sealand Road) 20,500; (Deva
Stadium) 5,987
(Total) Current Capacity: 6,012 (3,284)
seated

Visiting Supporters' Allocation: 1,896
maximum (seated 600 maximum)
Club Colours: Blue/White striped shirts, Blue
shorts
Nearest Railway Station: Chester (three miles)
Parking (Car): Car park at ground
Parking(Coach/Bus): Car park at ground
Police Force and Tel No: Cheshire (01244
350222)
Disabled Visitors' Facilities:
  Wheelchairs: West and East Stand
  Blind: Facility Available
Anticipated Development(s):

KEY
C Club Offices
S Club Shop
E Entrance(s) for visiting
    supporters
R Refreshment bars for visiting
    supporters
T Toilets for visiting supporters

↑ North direction (approx)

❶ Bumpers Lane
❷ To City centre and Chester
   railway station (1.5 miles)
❸ Car park

Above: 697211; *Right:* 697204

Newly promoted Chester City faced an early crisis in the team's newly-restored League status when, before the first ball of the new season was kicked, Mark Wright announced his departure from the Deva Stadium hot-seat. The club moved quickly to fill the vacancy, appointing the experienced Ray Matthias as caretaker. Towards the end of August, it was announced that ex-Liverpool star, Ian Rush, who numbered Chester amongst his earlier teams, was taking over at the Deva Stadium. The club struggled in its first season back in the Football League and, in early April, it was announced that Rush's assistant, Mark Aizlewood, had been sacked. This led Rush to announce his own resignation, frustrated at Aizlewood's dismissal and at the club's inability to allow for the squad to be strengthened.

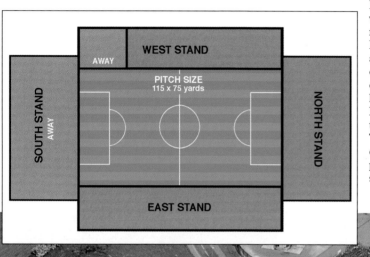

Following Rush's departure, it was announced later in the month that ex-Mansfield boss Keith Curle would take over as manager with a one-year contract. Curle faces a severe challenge in 2005/06 in keeping the club in the League; as one of a number of teams just above the League Two drop-zone the margin for error isn't great and it's probable that City will again struggle to stay up.

CHESTERFIELD

Recreation Ground, Saltergate, Chesterfield, S40 4SX

Tel No: 01246 209765
Advance Tickets Tel No: 01246 209765
Fax: 01246 556799
Web Site: www.chesterfield-fc.premiumtv.co.uk
E-Mail: reception@chesterfield-fc.co.uk
League: League One
Brief History: Found 1886. Former Ground: Spital Vale. Formerly named Chesterfield Town. Record attendance 30,968
(Total) Current Capacity: 8,504 (2,674 seated)
Visiting Supporters' Allocation: 2,200 maximum (maximum 800 seated)
Club Colours: Blue and white shirts, white shorts
Nearest Railway Station: Chesterfield
Parking (Car): Saltergate car park, street parking

Parking (Coach/Bus): As directed by Police
Police Force and Tel No: Derbyshire (01246 220100)
Disabled Visitors' Facilities:
  Wheelchairs: Saltergate Stand
  Blind: No special facility
Anticipated Development(s): The club's supporters voted in favour of relocation in the summer of 2003 and the club is now actively pursuing relocation to the site of the former Dema glassworks about one mile from the town centre with Alfred McAlpine as the proposed contractor. Assuming that the necessary planning permission is granted, the 10,000-seat ground should be completed in early 2007.

KEY

C Club Offices
S Club Shop
E Entrance(s) for visiting supporters
R Refreshment bars for visiting supporters
T Toilets for visiting supporters

↑ North direction (approx)

❶ Saltergate
❷ Cross Street
❸ St Margaret's Drive
❹ West Bars
❺ To A617 & M1 Junction 29
❻ To station and town centre
❼ Compton Street Terrace
❽ Cross Street End (away)

Above: 695552; Right: 695550

A much-improved season for the Spireites saw Chesterfield achieve the club's highest league finish for some six seasons — 17th in League One. Under the experienced Roy McFarland the season started well and at one stage it looked as though a Play-Off place was a real possibility. A post-Christmas slump, however, saw the team gradually drift down the table. Constrained by financial considerations, McFarland only possesses a small squad and this may well limit the club's ambitions on the field. Perhaps, in 2005/06, the best that the Saltergate faithful can hope for is to better the 17th place; the reality may be, however, that the club will face a battle to retain its League One status again.

COLCHESTER UNITED

Layer Road Ground, Colchester, CO2 7JJ

Tel No: 0871 226 2161
Advance Tickets Tel No: 087 226 2161
Fax: 01206 715327
Web Site: www.cu-fc.premiumtv.co.uk
E-Mail: commercial@colchesterunited.net
League: League One
Brief History: Founded 1937, joined Football League 1950, relegated 1990, promoted 1992. Record attendance 19,072
(Total) Current Capacity: 7,556 (1,877 seated)
Visiting Supporters' Allocation: 650 in Layer Road End (standing) plus 200 seats (East Coast Cable Stand)
Club Colours: Royal blue and white shirts, blue shorts
Nearest Railway Station: Colchester Town

Parking (Car): Street parking
Parking (Coach/Bus): Boadicea Way
Police Force and Tel No: Essex (01206 762212)
Disabled Visitors' Facilities:
  Wheelchairs: Space for 12 in front of terrace (next to Main Stand)
  Blind: Space for 3 blind persons and 3 guides (two regularly occupied by home supporters)
Anticipated Development(s): The club's plans for relocation to a new stadium at Cuckoo Farm in the spring of 2007 received a boost in January when it was confirmed that John Prescott had decided not to call in the planning application for the work. The next stage is for formal approval by Colchester Borough Council and for a funding and construction package to be put together.

KEY

C Club Offices
S Club Shop
E Entrance(s) for visiting supporters
R Refreshment bars for visiting supporters
T Toilets for visiting supporters

↑ North direction (approx)

❶ B1026 Layer Road
❷ Town Centre & Colchester Town BR Station (2 miles)
❸ Evening Gazette Main Stand
❹ Barside Popular Side
❺ East Coast Cable Stand

Above: 697285; Right: 697277

United, having finished the 2003/04 season in 11th place, were optimistic that 2004/05 would see the club better that performance. Unfortunately, in the league, Phil Parkinson's team underperformed, partly as a result of injuries and the loss of key players, and finished a disappointing 15th. Better form, however, was shown in cup competitions where the team reinforced its reputation as a giantkiller by defeating Premiership outfit West Brom at Layer Road 2-1 after extra time in the second round of the Carling Cup. For 2005/06, the club could struggle as Parkinson may well find it difficult to retain a number of his more talented players. Perhaps a season of mid-table safety is the best that the Layer Road faithful can look forward to.

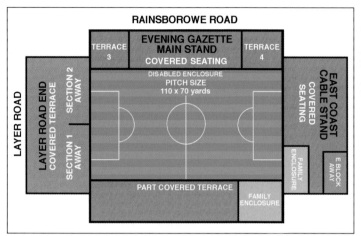

COVENTRY CITY

The Ricoh Arena, Judds Lane, Foleshill, Coventry CV6 6AQ

Telephone: 0870 421 1987
Advance Tickets Tel No: 0870 421 1987
Fax: 0870 421 5073
Web Site: www.ccfc.premiumtv.co.uk
E-mail: info@ccfc.co.uk
League: League Championship
Brief History: Founded 1883 as Singers FC, changed name to Coventry City in 1898. Former grounds: Dowell's Field, Stoke Road Ground and Highfield Road (1899-2005) moved to new ground for start of the 2005/06 season. Record attendance (at Highfield Road): 51,455
(Total) Current Capacity: 32,500
Visiting Supporters' Allocation: tbc
Club Colours: sky blue shirts, sky blue shorts
Nearest Railway Station: Coventry (three miles)

Parking (Car): As directed
Parking (Coach/Bus): As directed
Police Force and Tel No: West Midlands (02476 539010)
Disabled Visitors' Facilities:
   Wheelchairs: tbc
   Blind: tbc
Anticipated Development(s): The new season is the club's first at the new Ricoh Arena although it is unlikely that the ground will be completed for the start of the season and the club has applied to the League to play its opening games away from home. Although initial plans for the stadium included provision for a railway station (on the Coventry-Nuneaton), this part of the development has not as yet been progressed.

KEY

↑ North direction (approx)

❶ Judds Lane
❷ Rowley's Green Lane
❸ A444 Phoenix Way
❹ To Coventry city centre and BR railway station (three miles)
❺ Coventry-Nuneaton railway line
❻ To M6 Junction 3 (one mile) and Nuneaton
❼ Marconi West Stand
❽ Coventry Evening Telegraph North Stand
❾ NTL East Stand
❿ Jewson South Stand
⓫ Exhibition hall and planned casino

Above: 698849; *Right:* 698847

The last season at Highfield Road proved something of a disappointment to City fans, although the old ground was given a rousing farewell in the final league game to be played there with City defeating high-flying Derby County 6-2. Following a run of four defeats, culminating with a 2-1 home defeat against Leeds United, that left the Sky Blues in 20th position in the League Championship, it was announced in early January that Peter Reid was vacating the manager's seat 'by mutual consent' after 31 games in charge. In the short term he was replaced as caretaker boss by first-team coach Adrian Heath but the club moved quickly to appoint ex-Leicester City boss Micky Adams to oversee the team's final months at Highfield Road. Under Adams the team managed to remain above the drop zone — just. However, finishing in 19th position only two points above relegated Gillingham indicates the scale of the problem that Adams faces in the forthcoming campaign. Whilst the new ground should give the club a lift, there will need to be a major improvement on the field if City are to make a serious challenge to reclaim its spot in the Premiership.

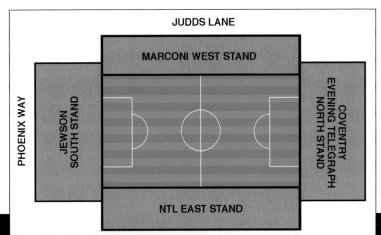

CREWE ALEXANDRA

The Alexandra Stadium, Gresty Road, Crewe, Cheshire, CW2 6EB

Tel No: 01270 213014
Advance Tickets Tel No: 01270 252610
Fax: 01270 216320
Website: www.crewealex.premtv.co.uk
E-Mail: info@crewealex.premiertv.co.uk
League: League Championship
Brief History: Founded 1877. Former Grounds:
Alexandra Recreation Ground (Nantwich Road),
Earle Street Cricket Ground, Edleston Road, Old
Sheds Fields, Gresty Road (Adjacent to current
Ground), moved to current Ground in 1906.
Founder members of 2nd Division (1892) until
1896. Founder members of 3rd Division North
(1921). Record attendance 20,000
(Total) Current Capacity: 10,100 all seated
Visiting Supporters' Allocation: 1,694 (Blue Bell
BMW Stand)

Club Colours: Red shirts, white shorts
Nearest Railway Station: Crewe
Parking (car): There is a car park adjacent to
the ground. It should be noted that there is a
residents' only scheme in operation in the
streets surrounding the ground.
Parking (Coach/Bus): As directed by Police
Police Force and Tel No: Cheshire (01270
500222)
Disabled Visitors' Facilities:
Wheelchairs: Available on all four sides
Blind: Commentary available
Anticipated Development(s): The club has
long term plans for the construction of a new
two-tier stand to replace the Blue Bell (BMW)
Stand, although there is no confirmed
timescale for the work.

KEY

C Club Offices
S Club Shop
E Entrance(s) for visiting
supporters

↑ North direction (approx)

❶ Crewe BR Station
❷ Gresty Road
❸ Gresty Road
❹ A534 Nantwich Road
❺ To A5020 to M6 Junction 16
❻ To M6 Junction 17 [follow
directions at roundabout to
M6 J16/J17]
❼ Main (Air Products) Stand
❽ Gresty Road (Advance
Personnel) Stand
❾ Charles Audi Stand
❿ Ringways Stand
(Blue Bell BMW)(away)
⓫ Car Park

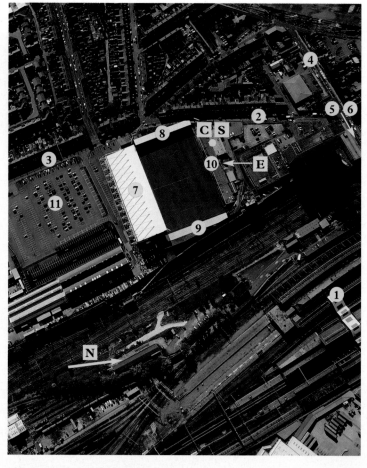

Above: 699095; *Right:* 699100

A season that had seemed promising early on, with the team even threatening to make a challenge for the Play-Offs, crumbled rapidly in the second half as the team tumbled rapidly down the Championship table. Each season there always seems to be one side that starts well and loses form and ends up being relegated and, in 2004/05, it looked as though it was going to be Dario Gradi's team. Indeed, as the last Sunday of the season dawned, Crewe looked destined to join Rotherham and Forest in League One. However, results on the day, with Crewe defeating Coventry allied to Gillingham's draw at Forest, resulted in Gradi's team surviving by goal difference. Undoubtedly the loss of Dean

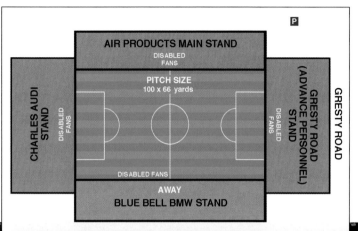

Ashton, transferred to Norwich in January, was a factor in the club's decline in the second half of the season and Gradi's challenge will be to find a player capable of scoring at this level as well as plugging the leaky defence that conceded no fewer than 86 goals — the worst record in this division by a considerable margin. Unless the squad is strengthened, it's hard to escape the conclusion that 2005/06 will again be a traumatic season at Gresty Road.

CRYSTAL PALACE

Selhurst Park, London, SE25 6PU

Tel No: 020 8768 6000
Advance Tickets Tel No: 08712 000071
Fax: 020 8771 5311
Web Site: www.cpfc.premiumtv.co.uk
E-Mail: info@cpfc.co.uk
Ticket Office/Fax: 020 8653 4708
League: League Championship
Brief History: Founded 1905. Former Grounds:
The Crystal Palace (F.A. Cup Finals venue),
London County Athletic Ground (Herne Hill),
The Nest (Croydon Common Athletic Ground),
moved to Selhurst Park in 1924. Founder
members 3rd Division (1920). Record attendance
51,482
(Total) Current Capacity: 26,400 all seated
Visiting Supporters' Allocation: Approx 2,000 in
Arthur Wait Stand
Club Colours: Blue and red striped shirts, blue
shorts

Nearest Railway Station: Selhurst, Norwood
Junction and Thornton Heath
Parking (Car): Street parking and Sainsbury's car
park
Parking (Coach/Bus): Thornton Heath
Police Force and Tel No: Metropolitan (020 8653
8568)
Disabled Visitors' Facilities:
Wheelchairs: 56 spaces in Arthur Wait and
Holmesdale Stands
Blind: Commentary available
Anticipated Development(s): Although the club
had plans to reconstruct the Main Stand —
indeed had Planning Permission for the work —
local opposition has meant that no work has been
undertaken. Serious thought is now being given
to relocation.

KEY
C Club Offices
S Club Shop
E Entrance(s) for visiting
supporters
T Toilets for visiting supporters

↑ North direction (approx)

❶ Whitehorse Lane
❷ Park Road
❸ A213 Selhurst Road
❹ Selhurst BR Station (1/2 mile)
❺ Norwood Junction BR
Station (1/4 mile)
❻ Thornton Heath BR Station
(1/2 mile)
❼ Car Park (Sainsbury's)

Above: 695773; Right: 695766

Promoted through the Play-Offs at the end of the 2003/04 season, few gave Iain Dowie's team much of a chance of avoiding an automatic return to the League Championship, considering that 12 months earlier, prior to Dowie's appointment, the team had been close to the relegation zone in the old First Division. It is to Dowie's credit, and to the team spirit engendered, that the team battled to the end. For the first season in the Premier League's history, the final games of the season saw no team as yet relegated and for much of the day it seemed as though the Eagles would pull off one of the great escapes in footballing history. Unfortunately, it wasn't to be as a late equaliser in the team's away match at Charlton meant that West Brom were saved and Palace consigned to the League Championship. It seems inevitable that Dowie's squad will be broken up, with top scorer Andy Johnson almost certain to depart and others, no doubt, will follow. Provided, however, that Dowie can keep the bulk of the team together then there is every possibility that the Eagles may yet soar again although probably the Play-Offs are the best that fans can hope for.

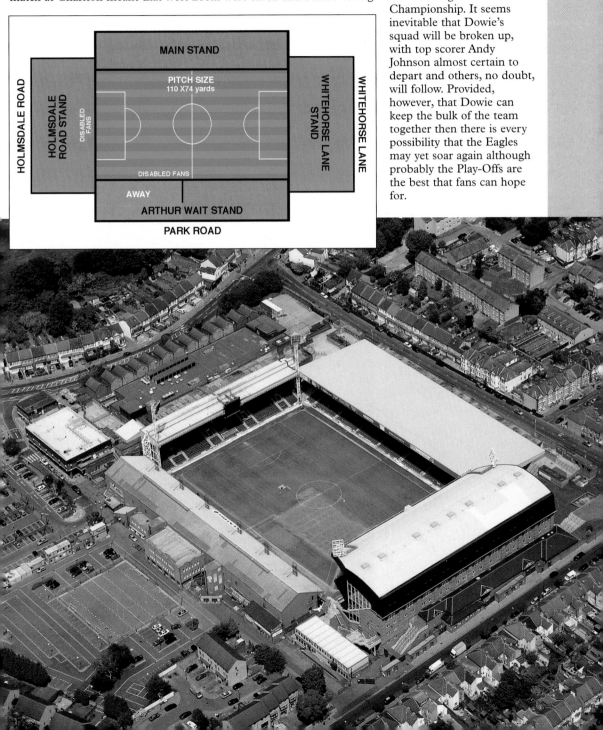

DARLINGTON

The Williamson Motors Stadium, Neasham Road, Darlington DL2 1GR

Tel No: 01325 387000
Advance Tickets Tel No: 01325 387030
Fax: 01325 387050
Web Site: www.darlington-fc.premiumtv.co.uk
E-mail: enquiries@darlington-fc.net
League: League Two
Brief History: Founded 1883. Founder members of 3rd Division (North) 1921. Relegated from 4th Division 1989. Promoted from GM Vauxhall Conference in 1990. Previous Ground: Fathoms; moving to Neasham Road in 2003. Record attendance (at Feethams) 21,023; (at Neasham Road) 11,600
(Total) Current Capacity: 27,500
Visiting Supporters' Allocation: 3,000 in East Stand

Club Colours: White and black shirts, black shorts
Nearest Railway Station: Darlington Bank Top
Parking (Car): Spaces available in adjacent car park (£5.00 fee)
Parking (Coach/Bus): As directed
Police Force and Tel No: Durham (01235 467681)
Disabled Visitors Facilities:
  Wheelchairs: 165 places
  Blind: No special facility
Anticipated Developments: With the construction of the new ground, there are no further plans for development as the existing ground's capacity is more than adequate for League Two.

KEY

⬆ North direction (approx)

❶ A66
❷ To Stockton
❸ To A66(M) and A1(M)
❹ Neasham Road
❺ To Darlington town centre and railway station (one mile)
❻ To Neasham
❼ Snipe Lane
❽ East Stand (away)

Above: 695517; *Right:* 695507

Following the traumas of the 2003/04 season, when the club entered Administration and sailed close to the drop zone, any improvement on and off the field would have been welcomed by fans of the Quakers. In the event, despite being severely constrained by financial considerations, Dave Hodgson's team performed well and came within a whisker of securing a Play-Off position. Unfortunately, it all came down to the last day with both Northampton and Darlington battling for the all-important seventh place. Providing Darlington bettered the Cobblers' result it would be the former into the Play-Offs. Darlington duly defeated Cheltenham 3-1 at home but victory for Northampton, 3-0 over relegated Kidderminster, ensured that the latter would enter the Play-Offs on goal difference. However, provided that Hodgson can maintain the improvement into 2005/06, the team should again feature in the battle for promotion out of League Two

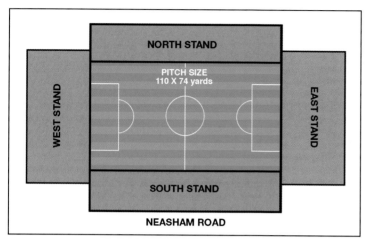

NORTH STAND

PITCH SIZE
110 X 74 yards

WEST STAND

EAST STAND

SOUTH STAND

NEASHAM ROAD

DERBY COUNTY

Pride Park, Derby, Derbyshire DE24 8XL

Tel No: 0870 444 1884
Advance Tickets Tel No: 0870 444 1884
Fax: 01332 667540
Web Site: www.dcfc.co.uk
E-Mail: derby.county@dcfc.co.uk
League: League Championship
Brief History: Founded 1884. Former grounds: The Racecourse Ground, the Baseball Ground (1894-1997), moved to Pride Park 1997. Founder members of the Football League (1888). Record capacity at the Baseball Ground: 41,826; at Pride Park: 33,597
(Total) Current Capacity: 33,597
Visiting Supporters' Allocation: 4,800 maximum in the South Stand
Club Colours: White shirts and black shorts

Nearest Railway Station: Derby
Parking (Car): 2,300 places at the ground designated for season ticket holders. Also two 1,000 car parks on the A6/A52 link road. No on-street parking
Parking (Coach/Bus): As directed
Police Force and Tel No: Derbyshire (01332 290100)
Disabled Visitors' Facilities:
  Wheelchairs: 70 home/30 away spaces
  Blind: Commentary available
Anticipated Development(s): There are no definite plans for the further development of Pride Park following the completion of the southwest corner.

KEY
C Club Offices
S Club Shop
E Entrance(s) for visiting supporters

↑ North direction (approx)

❶ To Derby Midland BR station
❷ North Stand
❸ Toyota West Stand
❹ South (McArthur Glen) Stand (away)
❺ Bombardier East Stand
❻ Derwent Parade
❼ To A52/M1
❽ To City Centre and A6
❾ A52

Above: 697495; *Right:* 697485

Following the 2003/04 season, which saw George Burley's team battling against the drop, the 2004/05 campaign proved much more successful, although there were occasional blips (such as the 3-1 defeat away at Lincoln City in the first round of the Carling Cup). Although never strong enough to sustain a push for automatic promotion, the Rams secured fourth spot, and thus a place in the Play-Offs. Unfortunately, however, a 2-0 defeat away at Preston North End and a 0-0 draw at home meant that the team from Lancashire headed off to the Millennium Stadium for a showdown with West Ham. Thus League Championship football will again be on offer at Pride Park in 2005/06. In early June it was announced that Burley was resigning as manager, claiming that his position was 'untenable'. Whilst the new manager, Phil Brown, will undoubtedly lose some of his squad during the close season, with Tom Huddlestone already on the move to Tottenham, there was sufficient progress on the field during last season to suggest that the team will again feature in the promotion battle in 2005/06.

DONCASTER ROVERS

The Earth Stadium, Belle Vue, Bawtry Road, Doncaster, DN4 5HT

Tel No: 01302 539441
Advance Tickets Tel No: 01302 379329
Fax: 01302 539679
Web Site: www.doncasterroversfc.premiumtv.co.uk
E-mail: info@doncasterroversfc.co.uk
League: League One
Brief History: Founded 1879, Former grounds: Town Moor, Belle Vue (not current ground), Deaf School Playing Field (later name Intake Ground), Bennetthorpe, moved to Belle Vue (former name Low Pasture) in 1922. Returned to Football League after a five-year absence in 2003. Record attendance 37,149
(Total) Current Capacity: 10,550 (1,157 seated)
Visiting Supporters' Allocation: 2,400 on Rossington End terrace (open, standing), plus 900 (300 seated) in Main Stand if required
Club Colours: Red and white shirts, red shorts

Nearest Railway Station: Doncaster
Parking (Car): Car park at ground
Parking (Coach/Bus): Car park at ground
Other Clubs Sharing Ground: Doncaster Dragons RLFC and Doncaster Belles Ladies FC
Police Force and Tel No: South Yorkshire (01302 366744)
Disabled Visitors' facilities:
　Wheelchairs: Bawtry Road
　Blind: No special facility
Anticipated Development(s): The council is involved in developing a £32 million community stadium that will provide a 15,000-seat ground (with the potential to extend this to 20,000 if required). The ground, which will also be used by the town's Rugby League team, is scheduled for completion by the start of the 2006/07 season.

KEY

↑ North direction (approx)

❶ Doncaster Racecourse
❷ A638 Bawtry Road
❸ To Bawtry
❹ To Doncaster town centre and railway station (1.5 miles)
❺ Carr House Road
❻ Car Park
❼ Main Stand
❽ Rossington End (away)

68

Above: 695664; *Right:* 695660

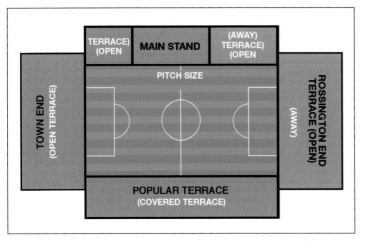

TERRACE) (OPEN	MAIN STAND	(AWAY) TERRACE) (OPEN

PITCH SIZE

TOWN END (OPEN TERRACE)

ROSSINGTON END TERRACE (OPEN) (AWAY)

POPULAR TERRACE (COVERED TERRACE)

Two promotions in two seasons often suggest that a team might struggle at the higher level but Dave Penney's Doncaster outfit confounded the pundits that suggested that the team might struggle to survive in League One. Whilst never being strong enough to suggest that a place in the Play-Offs was a possibility, Rovers finished in 10th only some five points off Hartlepool in sixth. For the new season, Rovers should again easily ensure their League One status and, with a slight improvement, could make a more sustained challenge for the Play-Offs.

EVERTON

Goodison Park, Goodison Road, Liverpool, L4 4EL

Tel No: 0151 330 2200
Advance Tickets Tel No: 0151 330 2300
Fax: 0151 286 9112
Web Site: www.evertonfc.com
E-Mail: everton@evertonfc.com
League: F.A. Premier
Brief History: Founded 1879 as St. Domingo, changed to Everton in 1880. Former grounds: Stanley Park, Priory Road and Anfield (Liverpool F.C. Ground), moved to Goodison Park in 1892. Founder-members Football League (1888). Record attendance 78,299
(Total) Current Capacity: 40,170 all seated
Visiting Supporters' Allocation: 3,000 (part of Bullens Road Stand) maximum
Club Colours: Blue and white shirts, white shorts
Nearest Railway Station: Liverpool Lime Street
Parking (Car): Corner of Utting Avenue and Priory Road

Parking (Coach/Bus): Priory Road
Police Force and Tel No: Merseyside (0151 709 6010)
Disabled Visitors' Facilities:
 Wheelchairs: Bullens Road Stand
 Blind: Commentary available
Anticipated Development(s): Having abandoned earlier proposals to relocate to a new stadium in the King's Dock area, the club is still keen to move from Goodison and is now investigating the possibility of constructing a 55,000-seat stadium in the Central docks area. This is, however, only a tentative proposal at this stage and much will depend on getting the funding in place. Another recent proposal is for the club to share Liverpool FC's planned new ground. Expect Everton to remain at Goodison for probably two or three seasons at least.

KEY

C Club Offices
S Club Shop
E Entrance(s) for visiting supporters
R Refreshment bars for visiting supporters
T Toilets for visiting supporters

↑ North direction (approx)

❶ A580 Walton Road
❷ Bullen Road
❸ Goodison Road
❹ Car Park
❺ Liverpool Lime Street BR Station (2 miles)
❻ To M57 Junction 2, 4 and 5
❼ Stanley Park

Above: 695687; *Right:* 695678

Whilst the start of the 2004/05 season was perhaps overshadowed by the transfer of Wayne Rooney to Manchester United, David Moyes' Everton shrugged off the loss of one of the country's best young players to make significant progress in the Premiership, pipping Liverpool to the all-important fourth position and thereby guaranteeing entry into the preliminary phase of the Champions League. Moyes' success with the squad was to bring him recognition as Manager of the Year but the scale of his task, if he wishes to see the team challenge the top three, was made evident in the penultimate game of the season when the Toffees crashed 7-0 away at Highbury. With the dominance of the top three almost guaranteed, it looks as though the competition for the rest of the Premier League will be for fourth position at best. Everton has the potential to challenge again for a UEFA Cup spot at least, but in 2005/06 there may well be better placed teams to grab fourth.

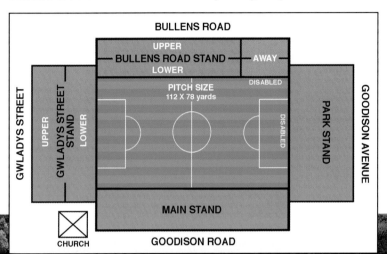

FULHAM

Craven Cottage, Stevenage Road, Fulham, London SW6 6HH

Club Offices: Fulham FC Training Ground, Motspur Park, New Malden, Surrey KT3 6PT
Tel No: 0870 442 1222
Advance Tickets Tel No: 0870 442 1234
Fax: 020 8336 0514
Web-site: www.fulhamfc.com
E-mail: enquiries@fulhamfc.com
League: F.A. Premier
Brief History: Founded in 1879 at St. Andrews Fulham, changed name to Fulham in 1898. Former grounds: Star Road, Ranelagh Club, Lillie Road, Eel Brook Common, Purer's Cross, Barn Elms, Half Moon (Wasps Rugby Football Ground), Craven Cottage (from 1894), moved to Loftus Road 2002 and returned to Craven Cottage for start of the 2004/05 season. Record Attendance: Craven Cottage (49,335)
(Total) Current Capacity: 22,000 (all seated)

Visiting Supporters' Allocation: 3,000 in Putney End
Club Colours: White shirts, black shorts
Nearest Railway Station: Putney Bridge (Tube)
Parking (Car): Street parking
Parking (Coach/Bus): Stevenage Road
Police Force and Tel No: Metropolitan (020 7741 6212)
Disabled Visitors' Facilities:
   Wheelchairs: Main Stand and Hammersmith End
   Blind: No special facility
Anticipated Development(s): Now restored to its traditional home at Craven Cottage, the club is looking either to further develop the ground with a view to obtaining an increased capacity. The most likely route is via the construction of corner infill stands and the rebuilding of the existing stands. There is, however, no confirmed timescale for this work.

KEY

E Entrance(s) for visiting supporters
R Refreshment bars for visiting supporters
T Toilets for visiting supporters

↑ North direction (approx)

❶ River Thames
❷ Stevenage Road
❸ Finlay Street
❹ Putney Bridge Tube Station (0.5 mile)
❺ Putney End (away)
❻ Riverside Stand
❼ Main Stand
❽ Hammersmith End
❾ Craven Cottage

Above: 699320; Right: 699315

A disappointing season for the Fulham faithful after the club's return to Craven Cottage. Chris Coleman's second season in charge proved to be less successful than the first with the team failing to sustain any sort of challenge after finishing the 2003/04 season in ninth position. Whilst never bad enough to be dragged into the relegation mire, Fulham certainly needed to be aware that the clubs below them were starting to pick up points. In the event, the team managed to drag itself to 14th place

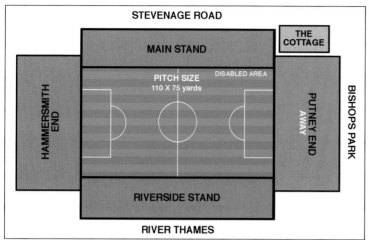

after an emphatic 6-0 victory over Norwich City in the last game of the season. However, Coleman and his squad can't afford to be complacent as both Sunderland and Wigan have the potential to make weaker existing Premier League teams struggle. Much will depend upon the squad that Coleman is able to retain or build for the new season, but another battle to stay in the Premier League can't be discounted.

GILLINGHAM

Priestfield Stadium, Redfern Avenue, Gillingham, Kent, ME7 4DD

Tel No: 01634 300000
Advance Tickets Tel No: 01634 300000
Fax: 01634 850986
Web Site: www.gillinghamfootballclub.premiumtv.co.uk
E-mail: info@priestfield.com
League: League One
Brief History: Founded 1893, as New Brompton, changed name to Gillingham in 1913. Founder-members Third Division (1920). Lost Football League status (1938), re-elected to Third Division South (1950). Record attendance 23,002
(Total) Current Capacity: 11,582 (all seated)
Visiting Supporters' Allocation: 1,300 (in Gillingham End)
Club Colours: Blue and black hooped shirts, blue shorts
Nearest Railway Station: Gillingham

Parking (Car): Street parking
Parking (Coach/Bus): As directed by Police
Police Force and Tel No: Kent (01634 234488)
Disabled Visitors' Facilities:
  Wheelchairs: Redfern Avenue (Main) Stand
  Blind: No special facility
Anticipated Development(s): The old open Town End Terrace was demolished during 2003 and replaced by a new temporary open stand. Planning Permission was granted in 2003 for the construction of a new 3,500-seat stand, to be named after noted fan the late Brian Moore, although work has yet to commence. Despite the investment at Priestfield, however, the club is investigating, in conjunction with the local council, the possibility of constructing a new stadium at Temple Marsh.

KEY

E Entrance(s) for visiting supporters

↑ North direction (approx)

❶ Redfern Avenue
❷ Toronto Road
❸ Gordon Road
❹ Gillingham BR station (¼ mile)
❺ Gordon Street Stand
❻ New two-tier Main (Medway) Stand
❼ New Rainham End Stand
❽ Gillingham End; uncovered seating (away)

Above: 697309; *Right:* 697302

With the Gills rooted in the Championship relegation zone at the end of November, Andy Hessenthaler stood down as manager although remaining with the club as a player (before being loaned out). Assistant John Gorman took over for one match — victory over fellow strugglers Nottingham Forest — before departing to the vacancy at Wycombe. In early December the experienced ex-Burnley boss, Stan Ternent, took over on a 30-month contract. Under the experienced Ternent it looked for much of the second half of the season as though the team would escape the drop. Unfortunately, however, results on the last day of the campaign — with Crewe defeating Coventry and Gillingham drawing away at already relegated Forest — saw Ternent's team relegated to League One on goal difference and, shortly after the end of the season, Ternent departed to be replaced by ex-Hartlepool boss Neale Cooper. As a relegated team, Gillingham will fancy their chances of making a quick return to the Championship, ironically as Crewe did a couple of seasons ago, but in recent years relegated teams have struggled to make an impact in League One. Perhaps a Play-Off place is possibly the best that the Priestfield faithful can look forward to.

GRIMSBY TOWN

Blundell Park, Cleethorpes, DN35 7PY

Tel No: 01472 605050
Advance Tickets Tel No: 01472 605050
Fax: 01472 693665
Web Site: www.grimsby-townfc.premiumtv.co.uk
E-Mail: enquiries@gtfc.co.uk
League: League Two
Brief History: Founded in 1878, as Grimsby Pelham, changed name to Grimsby Town in 1879. Former Grounds: Clee Park (two adjacent fields) and Abbey Park, moved to Blundell Park in 1899. Founder-members 2nd Division (1892). Record attendance 31,651
(Total) Current Capacity: 10,033 (all seated)
Visiting Supporters' Allocation: 2,200 in Osmond Stand
Club Colours: Black and white striped shirts, black shorts

Nearest Railway Station: Cleethorpes
Parking (Car): Street parking
Parking (Coach/Bus): Harrington Street
Police Force and Tel No: Humberside (01472 359171)
Disabled Visitors' Facilities:
  Wheelchairs: Harrington Street (Main) Stand
  Blind: Commentary available
Anticipated Development(s): The club's proposed relocation to a new £14 million stadium at Great Coates is proving problematic, with the latest difficulty being its inability to acquire the site. If the Great Coates scheme collapses, then the club will probably seek an alternative site for relocation.

KEY
C Club Offices
S Club Shop
E Entrance(s) for visiting supporters
R Refreshment bars for visiting supporters
T Toilets for visiting supporters

↑ North direction (approx)

❶ A180 Grimsby Road
❷ Cleethorpes BR Station (1½ miles)
❸ To Grimsby and M180 Junction 5
❹ Harrington Street
❺ Constitutional Avenue
❻ Humber Estuary

Above: 697766; Right: 697756

Following two successive relegations, the primary aim for new manager Russell Slade, in his first season, was to arrest the decline at Blundell Park and, in this somewhat limited ambition, he succeeded as the Mariners ultimately finished their League Two season in 18th position. Despite this lowly spot, however, the club was in fact closer, in point terms, to the Play-Offs than the relegation zone. Now that stability has been secured, Slade can look to the future and hope that the club's position will improve in 2005/06. Whilst automatic promotion may well be beyond the team, there is every possibility that the club could feature in the battle for the Play-Offs, although a top half finish is perhaps more realistic.

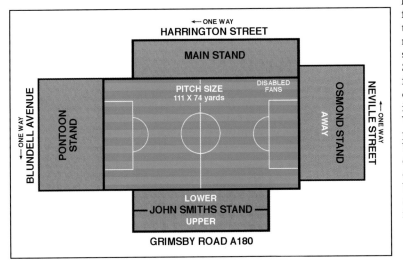

← ONE WAY
HARRINGTON STREET

MAIN STAND

PITCH SIZE
111 X 74 yards

DISABLED FANS

PONTOON STAND

OSMOND STAND
AWAY

← ONE WAY
BLUNDELL AVENUE

ONE WAY →
NEVILLE STREET

LOWER
— **JOHN SMITHS STAND** —
UPPER

GRIMSBY ROAD A180

HARTLEPOOL UNITED

Victoria Park, Clarence Road, Hartlepool, TS24 8BZ

Tel No: 01429 272584
Advance Tickets Tel No: 01429 272584
Fax: 01429 863007
Web Site: www.hartlepoolunited.premiumtv.co.uk
E-Mail: info@hartlepoolunited.co.uk
Fax: 01429 863007
League: League One
Brief History: Founded 1908 as Hartlepools
United, changed to Hartlepool (1968) and to
Hartlepool United in 1977. Founder-members
3rd Division (1921). Record attendance
17,426
(Total) Current Capacity: 7,629 (3,966 seated)
Visiting Supporters' Allocation: 1,000
(located in Rink Stand)
Club Colours: Blue and white striped shirts,
blue shorts

Nearest Railway Station: Hartlepool Church
Street
Parking (Car): Street parking and rear of clock
garage
Parking (Coach/Bus): As directed
Police Force and Tel No: Cleveland (01429
221151
Disabled Visitors' Facilities:
Wheelchairs: Cyril Knowles Stand and Rink
End
Blind: Commentary available
Anticipated Development(s): The plans for
the redevelopment of the Millhouse Stand are
still progressing, although there is now no
definite timescale. When this work does
commence, the ground's capacity will be
reduced to 5,000 temporarily.

KEY

C Club Offices
S Club Shop
E Entrance(s) for visiting
supporters

↑ North direction (approx)

❶ A179 Clarence Road
❷ Hartlepool Church Street BR
Station
❸ Marina Way
❹ Site of former Greyhound
Stadium
❺ To Middlesbrough A689 &
A1(M)
❻ To A19 North
❼ Rink End Stand

Above: 695504; *Right:* 695500

In one of the more bizarre managerial departures, Neale Cooper departed the top job at Hartlepool in early May with the club on the point of securing a place in the Play-Offs. Linked to the vacancy at Dunfermline Athletic, Cooper had been manager at Hartlepool for almost two years, during which time the club had established itself in League One; he was replaced as caretaker by Martin Scott. Cooper's departure, however, did not divert the team from the necessity of ensuring its position in the Play-Offs, a draw at rivals Bournemouth being enough to see off Bristol City whose victory at Sheffield Wednesday was not enough to see the Bristol team pip Hartlepool for the final Play-Off position. Finishing in sixth place, Hartlepool faced Tranmere Rover in the Play-Off semi-finals. Victory over the two legs ensured a Millennium Stadium showdown with Sheffield Wednesday. Having gone 1-0 down, Hartlepool took a 2-1 lead during the second half, but the game turned in the 81st minute when Hartlepool were reduced to 10 men when Chris Westwood was sent off and when Wednesday scored from the resulting penalty. Although the game went to extra time, Wednesday scored two more to take the League Championship spot and leave Hartlepool to face football in League One again.

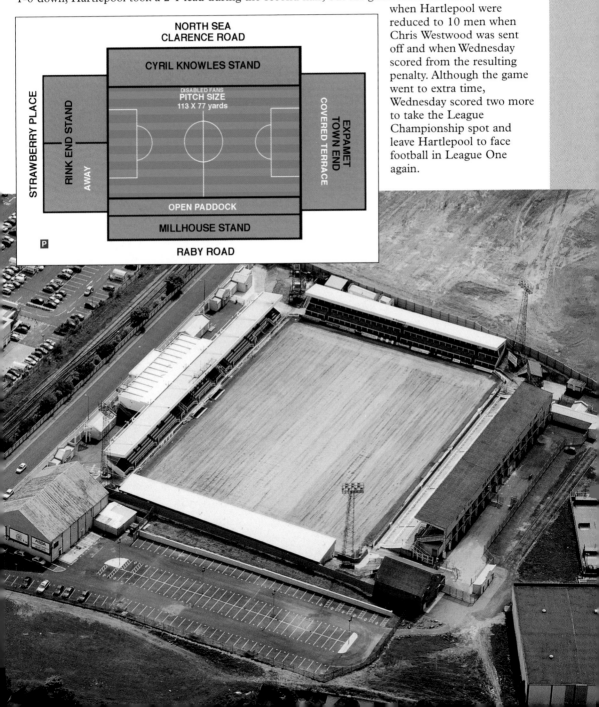

HUDDERSFIELD TOWN

The Galpharm Stadium, Leeds Road, Huddersfield, HD1 6PX

Tel No: 01484 484100
Advance Tickets Tel No: 01484 484123
Fax: 01484 484101
Web Site: www.htafc.premiumtv.co.uk
E-Mail: info@htafc.com
League: League One
Brief History: Founded 1908, elected to Football League in 1910. First Club to win the Football League Championship three years in succession. Moved from Leeds Road ground to Kirklees (Alfred McAlpine) Stadium 1994/95 season. Record attendance (Leeds Road) 67,037; Galpharm Stadium: 23,678
(Total) Current Capacity: 24,500 (all seated)
Visiting Supporters' Allocation: 4,037 (all seated)
Club Colours: Blue and white striped shirts, white shorts

Nearest Railway Station: Huddersfield
Parking (Car): Car parks (pre-sold) adjacent to ground
Parking (Coach/Bus): Car parks adjacent to ground
Other Clubs Sharing Ground: Huddersfield Giants RLFC
Police Force and Tel No: West Yorkshire (01484 422122)
Disabled Visitors' Facilities:
  Wheelchairs: Three sides of Ground, at low levels and raised area, including toilet access
  Blind: Area for Partially sighted with Hospital Radio commentary
Anticipated Development(s): With completion of the new North Stand, work on the Galpharm Stadium is over.

KEY
- **C** Club Offices
- **S** Club Shop
- **E** Entrance(s) for visiting supporters

↑ North direction (approx)

- ❶ To Leeds and M62 Junction 25
- ❷ A62 Leeds Road
- ❸ To Huddersfield BR station (1¼ miles)
- ❹ Disabled parking
- ❺ Town Avenue pay car park (on site of former ground)
- ❻ North Stand
- ❼ St Andrews pay car park
- ❽ Coach park
- ❾ South Stand (away)

Above: 695676; Right: 695671

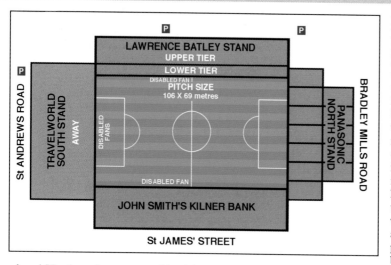

Promoted through the Play-offs at the end of 2003/04 Peter Jackson's Huddersfield took some time to acclimatise themselves to football at a higher level and, for a time, it looked as though the club would get dragged into the relegation mire. In the event, however, the team's form improved immeasurably in the second half of the season and ultimately the club came within a whisker of securing an unexpected Play-off place. Finishing in ninth, but only one point off sixth placed Hartlepool, was a considerable success and undoubtedly will see Town feature amongst the pre-season favourites for the promotion battle.

HULL CITY

Kingston Communications Stadium, Walton Street, Hull, East Yorkshire HU3 6HU

Tel No: 0870 837 0003
Advance Tickets Tel No: 0870 837 0004
Fax: 01482 304882
Web Site: www.hullcityafc.premiumtv.co.uk
E-mail: info@hulltigers.com
League: League Championship
Brief History: Founded 1904. Former grounds: The Boulevard (Hull Rugby League Ground), Dairycoates, Anlaby Road Cricket Circle (Hull Cricket Ground), Anlaby Road, Boothferry Park (from 1946). Moved to Kingston Communications Stadium in late 2002. Record attendance (at Boothferry Park) 55,019; (at Kingston Communications Stadium) 22,319
(Total) Current Capacity: 25,504 (all-seated)
Visiting Supporters' Allocation: 4,000 all-seated in North Stand
Club Colours: Amber and black striped shirts, black shorts

Nearest Railway Station: Hull Paragon
Parking (Car): There are 1,800 spaces on the Walton Street Fairground for use on match days
Parking (Coach/Bus): As directed
Other Clubs Sharing Ground: Hull RLFC
Police Force and Tel No: Humberside (01482 220148)
Disabled Visitors' facilities:
 Wheelchairs: c300 places
 Blind: contact club for details
Anticipated Development(s): The club moved into the new Kingston Communication Stadium towards the end of 2002. The ground is shared with Hull RLFC. The total cost of the 25,504-seat ground was £44million. The West Stand is provided with two tiers and there are plans for the construction of a second tier on the East and South Stands, taking the capacity to 34,000, if required.

KEY

↑ North direction (approx)

❶ A1105 Anlaby Road
❷ Arnold Lane
❸ West Stand
❹ East Stand
❺ Walton Street
❻ To city centre and railway station
❼ Car parks
❽ Railway line towards Scarborough
❾ Railway line towards Leeds
❿ A1105 westwards towards A63 and M62

Above: 695565; *Right:* 695561

Following promotion at the end of 2003/04 many expected Peter Taylor's City to take a season at least to acclimatise itself to football at League One level. In the event, however, the team was to prove one of the surprise packages and was to achieve automatic promotion to the League Championship well before the end of the season albeit pipped to the title by rivals Luton Town. With the capacity of the Kingston Communications Stadium allowing for greater crowds than at Boothferry Park, City have proved themselves to be capable of great things. However, experience with teams that have had two successive promotions suggests that a season of consolidation in 2005/06 might be the best that the City faithful can look forward to.

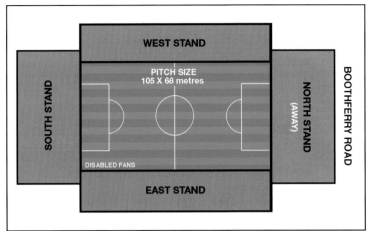

WEST STAND

PITCH SIZE
105 X 68 metres

SOUTH STAND

NORTH STAND
(AWAY)

BOOTHFERRY ROAD

DISABLED FANS

EAST STAND

IPSWICH TOWN

Portman Road, Ipswich, IP1 2DA

Tel No: 01473 400500
Advance Tickets Tel No: 0870 1110555
Fax: 01473 400040
Web Site: www.itfc.premiumtv.co.uk
E-Mail: enquiries@itfc.co.uk
League: League Championship
Brief History: Founded 1887 as Ipswich Association F.C., changed to Ipswich Town in 1888. Former Grounds: Broom Hill & Brookes Hall, moved to Portman Road in 1888. Record attendance 38,010
(Total) Current Capacity: 30,311 all seated
Visiting Supporters' Allocation: 2,280 all seated in Cobbold Stand
Club Colours: Blue shirts, white shorts
Nearest Railway Station: Ipswich

Parking (Car): Portman Road, Portman Walk & West End Road
Parking (Coach/Bus): West End Road
Police Force and Tel No: Suffolk (01473 611611)
Disabled Visitors' Facilities:
  Wheelchairs: Lower Britannia Stand
  Blind: Commentary available
Anticipated Development(s): The new Greene King (South) Stand has been followed by the construction of the new two-tier, 7,035-seat, North Stand, which was initially delayed as a result of legal action. The completion of the two stands takes Portman Road's capacity to more than 30,000.

KEY

C Club Offices
E Entrance(s) for visiting supporters
R Refreshment bars for visiting supporters
T Toilets for visiting supporters

⬆ North direction (approx)

❶ A137 West End Road
❷ Sir Alf Ramsay Way
❸ Portman Road
❹ Princes Street
❺ To Ipswich BR Station
❻ Car Parks
❼ Cobbold Stand
❽ Britannia Stand
❾ North Stand
❿ Greene King (South) Stand

Above: 698853; *Right:* 698862

Following the disappointment of losing in the Play-Offs in 2003/04, much was expected of Joe Royle's Ipswich Town in 2004/05 and the club lived up to expectations, threatening an automatic promotion spot right until the end of the campaign. In the event, Town's fate was ultimately determined on the last day of the season; Town needed to better Wigan Athletic's result to take second spot after already promoted Sunderland. Unfortunately, Wigan's 3-1 triumph over Reading rendered Ipswich's draw at Brighton meaningless and ensured that the team would again face the drama of the Play-Offs. In the first leg at Upton Park, Town came back from 2-0 down to draw 2-2 with the return leg at Portman Road to follow. However, come the return leg, only one team — West Ham — turned up and the Hammers' 2-0 victory ensures that Championship football is again on offer at Portman Road in 2005/06. In the coming campaign all three relegated teams look well capable to mounting a strong push for automatic promotion and so Town's best chance for promotion may well be through sneaking into the Play-Offs.

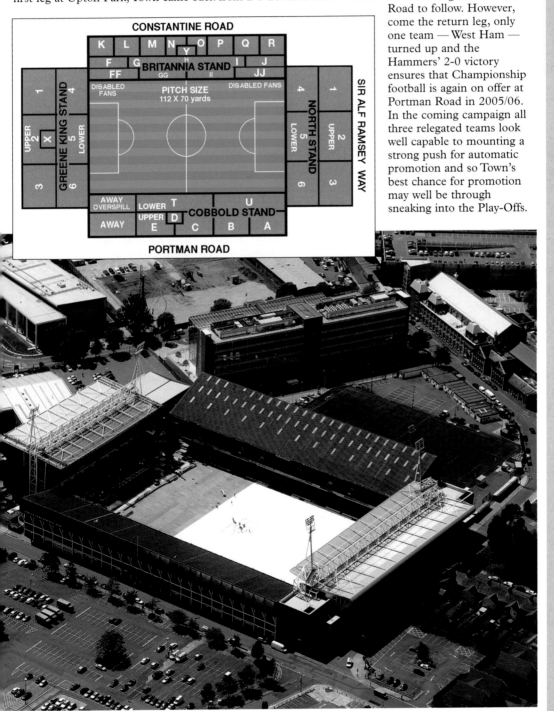

LEEDS UNITED

Elland Road, Leeds, LS11 0ES

Tel No: 0113 367 6000
Advance Tickets Tel No: 0845 121 1992
Fax: 0113 367 6050
Web Site: www.leedsunited.com
E-mail: admin@leedsunited.com
League: League Championship
Brief History: Founded 1919, formed from the former 'Leeds City' Club, who were disbanded following expulsion from the Football League in October 1919. Joined Football League in 1920. Record attendance 57,892
(Total) Current Capacity: 40,296 (all seated)
Visiting Supporters' Allocation: 1,725 in South East Corner (can be increased to 3,662 in South Stand if necessary)
Club Colours: White shirts, white shorts
Nearest Railway Station: Leeds City

Parking (Car): Car parks adjacent to ground
Parking (Coach/Bus): As directed by Police
Police Force and Tel No: West Yorkshire (0113 243 5353)
Disabled Visitors' Facilities:
 Wheelchairs: West Stand and South Stand
 Blind: Commentary available
Anticipated Development(s): Although the club had proposals for relocation to a new 50,000-seat stadium costing £60 million to be constructed close to the A1/M1 link road, given the club's high profile financial problems and recent relegation to the League Championship, it is unclear whether this work will proceed. The club has sold the Elland Road site and leased it back.

KEY
C Club Offices
S Club Shop
E Entrance(s) for visiting supporters

↑ North direction (approx)

❶ M621
❷ M621 Junction 2
❸ A643 Elland Road
❹ Lowfields Road
❺ To A58
❻ City Centre and BR station
❼ To M62 and M1

Above: 697482; Right: 697479

A season in which stability was the name of the game at Elland Road as the club sought both to establish itself in the League Championship, following relegation at the end of the 2003/04 season, and also to continue to reduce its enormous debts. In playing terms, United were neither threatened by relegation nor threatened to reach the Play-Offs and so Kevin Blackwall's team did perhaps as well as can be expected. A number of high profile players departed following relegation and, no doubt, more will leave during the close season, leaving the team with an unfamiliar feel to many. Off the field, the club's immediate financial woes were mitigated by the arrival of ex-Chelsea chairman Ken Bates. The new season represents Leeds' second season in the Championship and, at the end of it, the parachute payments from the Premier League will cease. A number of once famous clubs have found the struggle to return to top level football to be beyond them — just look at the number of ex-Premier League teams in League One — and it may well be that this season represents Leeds' best opportunity in the foreseeable future. However, it's hard to escape the conclusion that another season of mid-table mediocrity beckons.

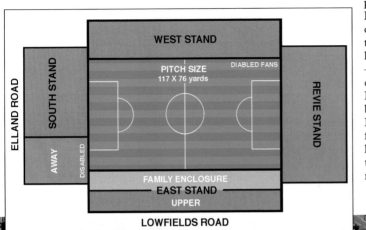

WEST STAND

ELLAND ROAD

SOUTH STAND

AWAY

DISABLED

PITCH SIZE
117 X 76 yards

DIABLED FANS

REVIE STAND

FAMILY ENCLOSURE
EAST STAND
UPPER

LOWFIELDS ROAD

LEICESTER CITY

Walkers Stadium, Filbert Way, Leicester, LE2 7FL

Tel No: 0870 040 6000
Advance Tickets Tel No: 0870 499 1884
Fax: 0116 291 1254
Web Site: www.lcfc.premiumtv.co.uk
E-mail: ticket.sales@lcfc.co.uk
League: League Championship
Brief History: Founded 1884 as Leicester Fosse, changed name to Leicester City in 1919. Former grounds: Fosse Road South, Victoria Road, Belgrave Cycle Track, Mill Lane, Aylstone Road Cricket Ground and Filbert Street (from 1891). The club moved to the new Walkers Stadium for the start of the 2002/03 season. Record attendance (at Filbert Street) 47,298; (at Walkers Stadium) 32,148
(Total) Current Capacity: 32,500
Visiting Supporters' Allocation: 3,000 (all seated) in North East of Ground

Club Colours: Blue shirts, white shorts
Nearest Railway Station: Leicester
Parking (Car): NCP car park
Parking (Coach/Bus): As directed
Police Force and Tel No: Leicester (0116 222 2222)
Disabled Visitors Facilities:
  Wheelchairs: 186 spaces spread through all stands
  Blind: Match commentary via hospital radio
Anticipated Developments: The club moved into the new 32,500-seat Walkers Stadium at the start of the 2002/03 season. Although there are no plans at present, the stadium design allows for the construction of a second tier to the East Stand, taking capacity to 40,000.

KEY

C Club Offices

↑ North direction (approx)

❶ Raw Dykes Road
❷ Eastern Road
❸ A426 Aylestone Road
❹ Freeman's Common Road
❺ To Lutterworth
❻ To city centre and railway station (one mile)
❼ Burnmoor Street
❽ River Soar
❾ Site of Filbert Street (old ground)

Above: 695615; Right: 695611

Following City's relegation from the Premiership at the end of 2003/04, the Foxes were widely considered to be amongst the pre-season favourites to bounce straight back. However, a relatively poor start to the campaign saw the club in mid-table in early October and, after more than two years in the post, Micky Adams resigned as manager in the middle of the month. Dave Bassett, the club's director of football, took over as caretaker before Craig Levein was appointed, moving from Hearts. Under Levein the club secured a disappointing, but safe, 15th place in the League Championship and the new manager has certainly laid the foundations for a more productive season in 2005/06. This, however, will be the Foxes' final season with the Premier League parachute payments and may well represent the club's best chance for a return to the Premier League. However, the three relegated teams look well placed to mount a serious challenge for the automatic promotion places and it may well be that Leicester's best chance will come through the Play-Offs.

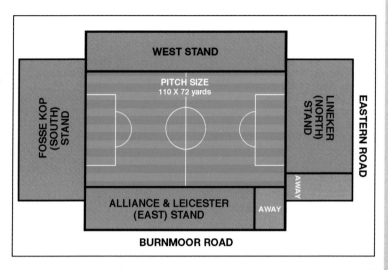

LEYTON ORIENT

Matchroom Stadium, Brisbane Road, Leyton, London, E10 5NF

Tel No: 020 8926 1111
Advance Tickets Tel No: 020 8926 1010
Fax: 020 8926 1110
Web Site: www.leytonorient.premiumtv.co.uk
E-Mail: info@leytonorient.net
League: League Two
Brief History: Founded 1887 as Clapton Orient, from Eagle Cricket Club (formerly Glyn Cricket Club formed in 1881). Changed name to Leyton Orient (1946), Orient (1966), Leyton Orient (1987). Former grounds: Glyn Road, Whittles Athletic Ground, Millfields Road, Lea Bridge Road, Wembley Stadium (2 games), moved to Brisbane Road in 1937. Record attendance 34,345
(Total) Current Capacity: 7,700 (all-seated)
Visiting Supporters' Allocation: 700 (all seated) in East Stand/Terrace
Club Colours: Red shirts, red shorts

Nearest Railway Station: Leyton (tube), Leyton Midland Road
Parking (Car): Street parking
Parking (Coach/Bus): As directed by Police
Police Force and Tel No: Metropolitan (020 8556 8855)
Disabled Visitors' Facilities:
  Wheelchairs: Windsor Road
  Blind: Match commentary supplied on request
Anticipated Development(s): The new West Stand, constructed during the 2004/05 season, adds 2,500 to the ground's capacity and also houses club offices and other facilities. This will increase the ground's capacity to 7,700 from the start of the 2005/06 season. The provision of rental office space in the West Stand is designed to raise income that will ultimately help fund the construction of a new North Stand, construction of which will see Brisbane Road's capacity increase to 10,000.

KEY

C Club Offices
S Club Shop
E Entrance(s) for visiting supporters

↑ North direction (approx)

❶ Buckingham Road
❷ Oliver Road
❸ A112 High Road Leyton
❹ To Leyton Tube Station (¼ mile)
❺ Brisbane Road
❻ Windsor Road
❼ To Leyton Midland Road BR station
❽ South Stand
❾ West Stand

Above: 699341; Right: 699328

At one stage, with Orient top of the League Two table in October, it looked as though Martin Ling's team might make a serious push either for automatic promotion or, at worst, a Play-Off place. Unfortunately, however, the early season form wasn't maintained, possibly as a result of injuries to key players such as Gary Alexander, and the team gradually slipped down the League Two table, ultimately finishing in a disappointing 11th position (albeit still a considerable improvement on the 19th achieved in 2003/04). Provided that the team can maintain its form for the season then, in 2005/06, Orient certainly has the potential to make a more determined push for the Play-Offs at least

OLIVER ROAD

WEST STAND

PITCH SIZE
115 X 80 yards

BUCKINGHAM ROAD

SOUTH STAND

WINDSOR ROAD

DISABLED FANS

AWAY ENCLOSURE | ENCLOSURE | WINGS

AWAY SEATS | EAST STAND

BRISBANE ROAD

LINCOLN CITY

Sincil Bank, Lincoln, LN5 8LD

Tel No: 0870 899 2005
Advance Tickets Tel No: 0870 899 2005
Fax: 01522 880020
Web Site: www.redimps.premiumtv.co.uk
E-Mail: lcfc@redimps.com
League: League Two
Brief History: Founded 1884. Former Ground: John O'Gaunts Ground, moved to Sincil Bank in 1895. Founder-members 2nd Division Football League (1892). Relegated from 4th Division in 1987, promoted from GM Vauxhall Conference in 1988. Record attendance 23,196
(Total) Current Capacity: 11,100 (all seated)
Visiting Supporters' Allocation: 2,000 in Co-op Community Stand (part, remainder for Home fans)

Club Colours: Red and white striped shirts, black shorts
Nearest Railway Station: Lincoln Central
Parking (Car): City centre car parks; limited on-street parking
Parking (Coach/Bus): South Common
Police Force and Tel No: Lincolnshire (01522 529911)
Disabled Visitors' Facilities:
Wheelchairs: The Simons and South (Mundy) Park stands
Blind: No special facility
Anticipated Development(s): Following the replacement of the seats in the Stacey West Stand, Sincil Bank is once again an all-seater stadium.

KEY
C Club Offices
S Club Shop
E Entrance(s) for visiting supporters

↑ North direction (approx)

❶ A46 High Street
❷ Sincil Bank
❸ Sausthorpe Street
❹ Cross Street
❺ Co-op Community Stand (away)
❻ A158 South Park Avenue
❼ Stacey West Stand
❽ Lincoln Central BR Station (1/2 mile)
❾ Family Stand

92
Above: 697261; *Right:* 697523

With Keith Alexander now restored to full-time management following his health scare during the 2003/04 season, much was expected from the Imps, having made the Play-Offs despite Alexander's absence, and in this fans were not to be disappointed. As before, whilst not strong enough to maintain a challenge for automatic promotion, the club secured a Play-Off position despite a last-day defeat at champions Yeovil Town. Drawn against Macclesfield Town in the Play-Off semi-finals, victory over the two legs meant that Alexander's team made the trip to Cardiff where the squad faced Southend in the Final. Unfortunately, despite having a goal ruled out for offside, Lincoln were to be beaten 2-0 after extra time, resulting in League Two football again at Sincil Bank in 2005/06. Alexander has promised that the squad will be overhauled in the summer in the hope of pushing for automatic promotion; if he succeeds in achieving a strengthened squad then there is every chance that the Imps will again be one of the teams to watch in League Two during 2005/06.

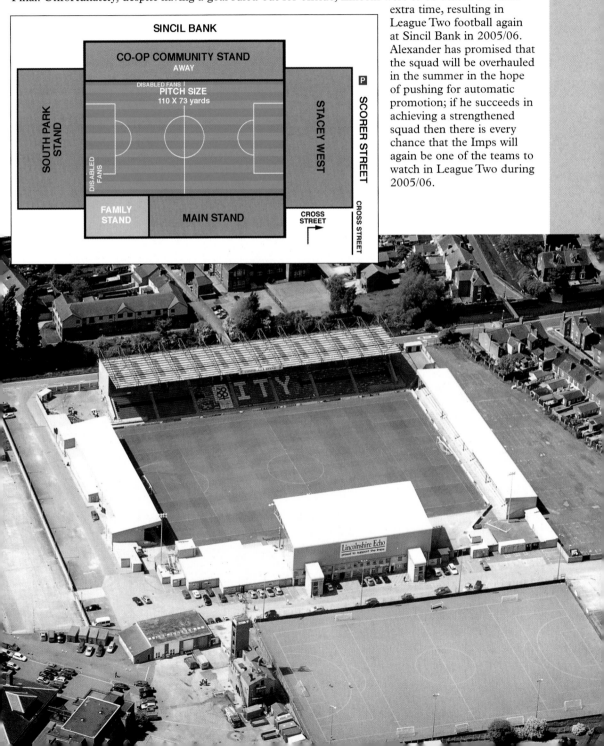

LIVERPOOL

Anfield Road, Liverpool, L4 0TH

Tel No: 0151 263 2361
Advance Tickets Tel No: 0870 220 2345
Fax: 0151 260 8813
Ticket Enquiries Fax: 0151 261 1416
Web Site: www.liverpoolfc.tv
League: F.A. Premier
Brief History: Founded 1892. Anfield Ground formerly Everton F.C. Ground. Joined Football League in 1893. Record attendance 61,905
(Total) Current Capacity: 45,362 (all seated)
Visiting Supporters' Allocation: 1,972 (all seated) in Anfield Road Stand
Club Colours: Red shirts, red shorts
Nearest Railway Station: Kirkdale
Parking (Car): Stanley car park
Parking (Coach/Bus): Priory Road and Pinehurst Avenue

Police Force and Tel No: Merseyside (0151 709 6010)
Disabled Visitors' Facilities:
  Wheelchairs: Kop and Main Stands
  Blind: Commentary available
Anticipated Development(s): The club was given formal approval by the local authority for the construction of the new ground in late July 2004. The project progressed further at the end of September 2004 when John Prescott gave his seal of approval. Work is scheduled to start on the new 55,000-seat stadium, which will retain the name Anfield, during 2005 with a scheduled completion date of the start of the 2007/08 season.

KEY
C Club Offices
S Club Shop

↑ North direction (approx)

❶ Car Park
❷ Anfield Road
❸ A5089 Walton Breck Road
❹ Kemlyn Road
❺ Kirkdale BR Station (1 mile)
❻ Utting Avenue
❼ Stanley Park
❽ Spion Kop
❾ Anfield Road Stand

Above: 695700; Right: 695692

How does one sum up Rafael Benitez's first season as manager at Anfield? Agony or ecstasy? On the one hand there was the agony of inconsistent league form, which saw Liverpool finish in fifth place and thus qualifying theoretically only for the UEFA Cup, the agony of defeat by Chelsea in the final of the Carling Cup at the Millennium Stadium and the agony of an embarrassing defeat at Championship side Burnley in the third round on the FA Cup. On the other hand there was the night of triumph in Istanbul when the team, against all the odds, triumphed in the final of the Champions League, defeating AC Milan on penalties after having come back from 3-0 down at half time. Returning to Merseyside with the trophy for the first time in 21 years, the team put behind them a series of domestic disappointment and established the current squad's place in the pantheon of Anfield heroes. For 2005/06 there are a number of questions that will need to be answered. Can Benitez retain the services of one or two of his most influential players, most notably Steven Gerrard? Will UEFA relax the rules and permit Liverpool to defend the trophy? Can the team avoid some of the crippling injuries that so afflicted Benitez's selections during 2004/05 with players such as Alonso and Cisse missing for much of the campaign? If the answers to one or more of these questions is 'yes' (as it is in the case of the defence of the Champions League), then Liverpool has again got the potential to become a serious force in domestic football and help convert the title battle into a four-horse race.

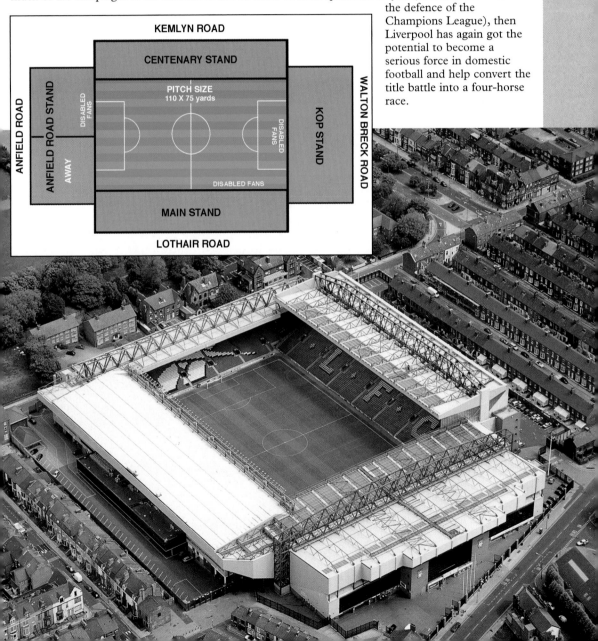

LUTON TOWN

Kenilworth Road Stadium, 1 Maple Road, Luton, LU4 8AW

Tel No: 01582 411622
Advance Tickets Tel No: 01582 416976
Fax: 01582 405070
Web Site: www.lutontown.premiumtv.co.uk
E-Mail: clubsec@lutontown.co.uk
League: League Championship
Brief History: Founded 1885 from an amalgamation of Wanderers F.C. and Excelsior F.C. Former Grounds: Dallow Lane & Dunstable Road, moved to Kenilworth Road in 1905. Record attendance 30,069
(Total) Current Capacity: 9,970 (all seated)
Visiting Supporters' Allocation: 2,200
Club Colours: Orange and blue shirts, blue shorts
Nearest Railway Station: Luton
Parking (Car): Street parking

Parking (Coach/Bus): Luton bus station
Police Force and Tel No: Bedfordshire (01582 401212)
Disabled Visitors' Facilities:
  Wheelchairs: Kenilworth Road and Main stands
  Blind: Commentary available
Anticipated Development(s): Towards the end of the 2003/04 season it was announced that the consortium that took the club out of Administration would progress with plans for relocation. The new stadium, to be located close to Junction 10 of the M1, would provide seating for 15,000. The anticipated time-scale is to have the new ground available within three years but nothing is as yet confirmed.

KEY

C Club Offices
S Club Shop
E Entrance(s) for visiting supporters
R Refreshment bars for visiting supporters
T Toilets for visiting supporters

↑ North direction (approx)

❶ To M1 Junction 11
❷ Wimborne Road
❸ Kenilworth Road
❹ Oak Road
❺ Dunstable Road
❻ Luton BR Station (1 mile)
❼ Ticket Office

Above: 695595; Right: 695588

A season of some success for Luton saw Mike Newell's team in the automatic promotion places from the start of the season and it came as no surprise that the time was to achieve both automatic promotion and the League One title. Promotion to the League Championship will bring new challenges, not least of which will be the opportunity to renew local rivalry with Watford. As with all promoted teams, Luton may well struggle to retain the newly-won status but confidence should be high and there are undoubtedly a number of Championship sides that are potentially weaker.

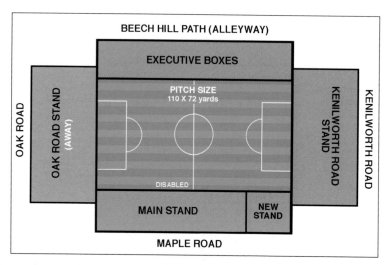

MACCLESFIELD TOWN

Moss Rose Ground, London Road, Macclesfield, SK11 7SP

Tel No: 01625 264686
Advance Tickets Tel No: 01625 264686
Fax: 01625 264692
Web Site: www.mtfc.premiumtv.co.uk
E-Mail: office@mtfc.co.uk
League: League Two
Brief History: Founded 1874. Previous ground: Rostron Field moved to Moss Rose Ground in 1891. Winners of the Vauxhall Conference in 1994/95 and 1997/97. Admitted to Football League for 1997/98 season. Record attendance 10,041
(Total) Current Capacity: 6,307 (2,561 seated)
Visiting Supporters' Allocation: 1,900 (1,500 in Silkman Terrace; 400 seated in Estate Road Stand)
Club Colours: Royal blue, royal blue shorts
Nearest Railway Station: Macclesfield
Parking (Car): No parking at the ground and the nearest off-street car park is in the town centre (25min walk). There is some on-street parking in the vicinity, but this can get crowded.
Parking (Coach/Bus): As directed
Police Force and Tel No: Cheshire (01625 610000)
Disabled Visitors' Facilities:
　Wheelchairs: 45 places in Estate Road Stand
　Blind: No special facility
Anticipated Development(s): The new Estate Road (Alfred McAlpine) Stand, with its 1,497 seats, was completed towards the end of the 2000/01 season and officially opened on 5 May 2001. This is the first phase of a scheme to redevelop Moss Rose; the next phase will see a seated second tier raised above the existing terrace at the Silkman End. Other recent work has included the provision of permanent toilets at the away end.

KEY

C Club Offices
E Entrance(s) for visiting supporters

↑ North direction (approx)

❶ A523 London Road
❷ To Town Centre and BR station (1.5 miles)
❸ To Leek
❹ Moss Lane
❺ Star Lane
❻ Silkmans Public House (now closed)
❼ Star Lane End
❽ Silkman End (away section)
❾ Estate Road Stand

Above: 697248; *Right:* 697237

As expected, the confirmation that the experienced Brian Horton was to remain as manager of the Silkmen in 2004/05 meant that the progress achieved on the field after his appointment in March 2004 continued into the new campaign. Whilst the team was not one of those strong enough to maintain a challenge for automatic promotion (not helped by the fact that the team failed to win any of its last four home games), the team was to finish in fifth place and thereby enter the Play-Offs. However, defeat over the two legs of the semi-finals means that Town will again be playing in League Two in 2005/06. Provided that the progress already made under Horton continues, then there is every possibility that the team will again challenge for the Play-Offs at least.

STAR LANE

STAR LANE STAND

ESTATE ROAD STAND

AWAY

PITCH SIZE
100 X 66 metres

AWAY
SILKMAN END
UNCOVERED

DISABLED FANS

UNCOVERED TERRACE

MAIN STAND

LONDON ROAD TERRACE UNCOVERED

A523 LONDON ROAD

MANCHESTER CITY

The City of Manchester Stadium, Sportcity, Manchester M11 3FF

Tel No: 0870 062 1894
Advance Tickets Tel No: 0870 062 1894
Fax: 0161 438 7999
Web Site: www.mcfc.co.uk
E-mail: mcfc@mcfc.co.uk
League: F.A. Premier
Brief History: Founded 1880 at West Gorton, changed name to Ardwick (reformed 1887) and to Manchester City in 1894. Former grounds: Clowes Street (1880-81), Kirkmanshulme Cricket Club (1881-82), Queens Road (1882-84), Pink Bank Lane (1884-87), Hyde Road (1887-1923) and Maine Road (from 1923 until 2003). Moved to the City of Manchester Stadium for the start of the 2003/04 season. Founder-members 2nd Division (1892). Record attendance (at Maine Road) 84,569 (record for a Football League Ground); at City of Manchester Stadium 47,304
(Total) Current Capacity: 48,000

Visiting Supporters' Allocation: 3,000 (South Stand); can be increased to 4,500 if required
Club Colours: Sky blue shirts, white shorts
Nearest Railway Station: Manchester Piccadilly
Parking (Car): Ample match day parking available to the north of the stadium, entrance via Alan Turing Way. On-street parking restrictions operate in all areas adjacent to the stadium on matchdays.
Parking (Coach/Bus): Coach parking for visiting supporters is adjacent to turnstiles at Key 103 Stand. For home supporters to the north of the stadium, entrance from Alan Turing Way.
Police Force and Tel No: Greater Manchester (0161 872 5050)
Disabled Visitors' facilities:
  Wheelchairs: 300 disabled seats around ground
  Blind: 14 places alongside helpers in East Stand Level 1. Commentary available via headsets.

KEY	
⬆	North direction (approx)
❶	A662 Ashton New Road
❷	Commonwealth Boulevard
❸	Stadium Way
❹	A6010 Alan Turing Way
❺	North Stand
❻	South (Key 103) Stand
❼	West (Colin Bell) Stand
❽	East Stand
❾	National Squash Centre
❿	Warm-up track
⓫	To Manchester city centre and Piccadilly station (1.5 miles)

Above: 697235; *Right:* 697226

In early March, following confirmation that he intended not to renew his contract as manager at the end of the 2004/05 season Kevin Keegan was another who learnt that the uncertainty arising from a pre-announced departure was such that his position was increasingly untenable. His position wasn't aided by defeat in the FA Cup at League One outfit Oldham, where City lost 1-0 in the Third Round. Thus, after some four years with City, which had seen the club recover its position in the Premiership and move to the new ground, Keegan departed; Stuart Pearce took over initially as caretaker. Following a string of reasonable results, which saw City climb the table, Pearce was confirmed in the managerial hot-seat before the end of the 2004/05 season. Under Pearce, there was a real possibility that European football could be achieved via the UEFA Cup. Ultimately, this depended upon results on the last Sunday of the season. Needing to beat Middlesbrough to finish in the all-important seventh place, City could only draw 1-1; even more galling was the fact that Robbie Fowler missed an injury time penalty that would have given City the valuable points. For 2005/06 City should again feature as one of the top-half teams. Never strong enough to challenge for the Champions League but certainly capable of going after a UEFA Cup spot.

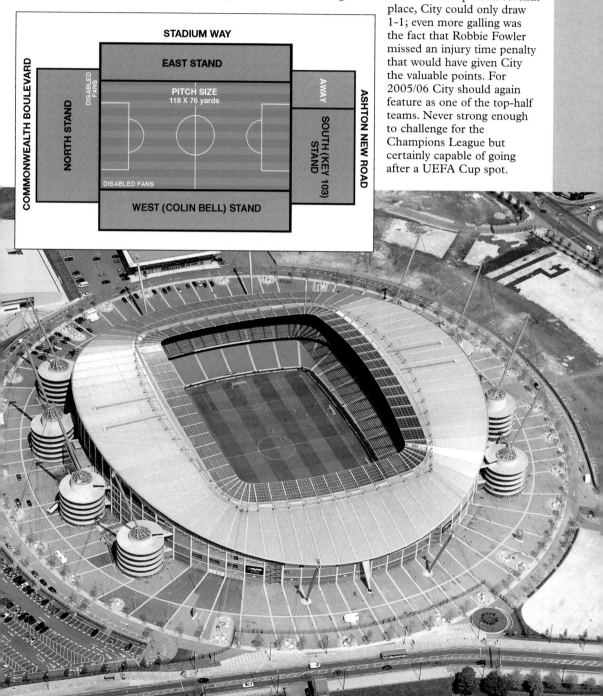

MANCHESTER UNITED

Old Trafford, Sir Matt Busby Way, Manchester, M16 0RA

Tel No: 0161 868 8000
Advance Tickets Tel No: 0870 442 1999
Fax: 0161 868 8804
Web Site: www.manutd.com
E-mail: enquiries@manutd.co.uk
League: F.A. Premier
Brief History: Founded in 1878 as 'Newton Heath L&Y', later Newton Heath, changed to Manchester United in 1902. Former Grounds: North Road, Monsall & Bank Street, Clayton, moved to Old Trafford in 1910 (used Manchester City F.C. Ground 1941-49). Founder-members Second Division (1892). Record attendance 76,962
(Total) Current Capacity: 68,174 (all seated)
Visiting Supporters' Allocation: Approx. 3,000 in corner of South and East Stands
Club Colours: Red shirts, white shorts

Nearest Railway Station: At Ground
Parking (Car): Lancashire Cricket Ground and White City
Parking (Coach/Bus): As directed by Police
Police Force and Tel No: Greater Manchester (0161 872 5050)
Disabled Visitors' Facilities:
 Wheelchairs: South East Stand
 Blind: Commentary available
Anticipated Development(s): The club was granted planning permission in early February for a £39million expansion of Old Trafford. This is intended to increase the ground's capacity to 76,000 by the start of the 2006/07 season and involves infilling the north-west and north-east corners of the ground. The proposals include improvements to the local public transport infrastructure.

KEY

C Club Offices

↑ North direction (approx)

❶ To A5081 Trafford Park Road to M63 Junction 4 (5 miles)
❷ A56 Chester Road
❸ Manchester Ship Canal
❹ To Old Trafford Cricket Ground
❺ To Parking and Warwick Road BR Station
❻ Sir Matt Busby Way

Above: 699110; Right: 699116

A season of drama both on and off the field saw United change hands with the US tycoon Malcolm Glazer assuming control in controversial circumstances in May. It's difficult at this stage to establish what the long-term implications of the takeover are, other than a club that was debt free is now saddled with significant borrowings as a result of the means by which Glazer secured his acquisition. Whilst United has been making a profit over recent years, it would seem doubtful if the existing level would be enough to support the supposed level of debt without either increasing ticket prices dramatically or by seeking alternative revenue through revised television rights. Whilst it would appear that the Glazers have offered money for strengthening the squad, fans remain dubious and United's headlines in 2005/06 may well be dominated by events off the field rather than on it. In terms of actual football, 2004/05 was again ultimately season of disappointment. Third in the Premier League and failure in the Champions League were compounded by defeat to Arsenal in the FA Cup final. In a match that United dominated, the Gunners were ultimately to triumph on penalties despite United's dominance during the 120min of actual play. For 2005/06 United will again be a force in the Premier League, but the club's best chance for silverware may well again come in one of the cup competitions. Much, however, will depend on events in the boardroom before the start of the new season.

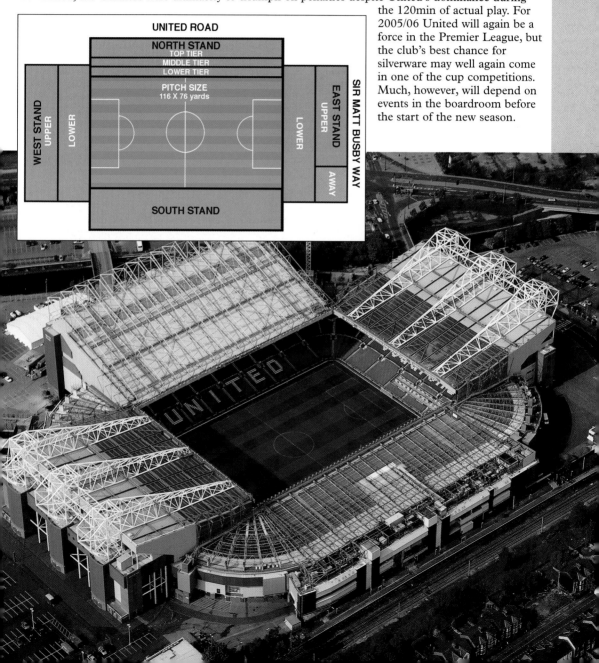

MANSFIELD TOWN

Field Mill Stadium, Quarry Lane, Mansfield, Notts, NG18 5DA

Tel No: 0870 756 3160
Advance Tickets Tel No: 0870 756 3160
Fax: 01623 482495
Web Site: www.mansfieldtown.premiumtv.co.uk
E-mail: stags@stags.plus.com
League: League Two
Brief History: Founded 1910 as Mansfield
Wesleyans Boys Brigade, changed to Mansfield
Town in 1914. Former Grounds: Pelham
Street, Newgate Lane and The Prairie, moved
to Field Mill in 1919. Record attendance
24,467
(Total) Current Capacity: 9,990 (all seated)
Visiting Supporters' Allocation: 1,800 (all
seated) in North Stand
Club Colours: Amber with blue trim shirts,
Blue shorts with amber trim

Nearest Railway Station: Mansfield
Parking (Car): Car park at Ground
Parking (Coach/Bus): Car park at Ground
Police Force and Tel No: Nottinghamshire
(01623 420999)
Disabled Visitors' Facilities:
Wheelchairs: Facilities provided in North,
West and South stands
Blind: No special facility
Anticipated Development(s): Work on the
Main Stand and on the North and Quarry
Lane ends was completed in early 2001,
leaving the Bishop Street Stand as the only
unreconstructed part of Field Mill. Plans exist
for this to be rebuilt as a 2,800-seat structure
but the time scale is unconfirmed.

KEY

E Entrance(s) for visiting
supporters

↑ North direction (approx)

❶ Car Park(s)
❷ Quarry Lane
❸ A60 Nottingham Road to
M1 Junction 27
❹ Portland Street
❺ To A38 and M1 Junction 28
❻ To Town Centre
❼ Mansfield railway station
❽ North Stand (away)
❾ Quarry Lane End (South
Stand)
❿ Bishop Street Stand
⓫ Main (West) Stand

Above: 698870; Right: 698878

Having failed in the Play-Offs in 2003/04, much was expected of the Stags in 2004/05 but, ultimately, the season was to prove disappointing, with the club finishing in 13th place well outside the Play-Offs. Partly, this was the result of the loss of key players in the close season but events off the field also had an effect. In mid-November, the club announced that Keith Curle had been suspended as manager, following alleged bullying of a trainee, and that ex-Stockport boss Carlton Palmer had take over as a temporary measure. In early March, once Curle's claims for unfair dismissal had been rejected, Palmer was confirmed as the Stags' new manager until 2006. Palmer has brought in new players and, provided that the team can gel, then there is every possibility that the club could again feature in the battle for the Play-Offs in 2005/06.

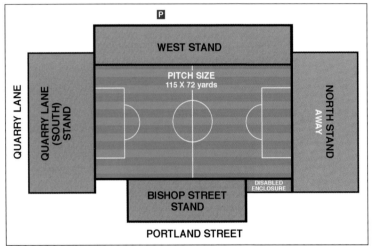

MIDDLESBROUGH

Riverside Stadium, Middlesbrough, Cleveland TS3 6RS

Tel No: 0870 421 1986
Advance Tickets Tel No: 0870 421 1986
Fax: 01642 877840
Web Site: www.mfc.co.uk
E-mail: media.dept@mfc.co.uk
League: F.A. Premier
Brief History: Founded 1876. Former Grounds: Archery Ground (Albert Park), Breckon Hill Road, Linthorpe Road, moved to Ayresome Park in 1903, and to current ground in Summer 1995. F.A. Amateur Cup winners 1894 and 1897 (joined Football League in 1899). Record attendance (Ayresome Park) 53,596, (Riverside Stadium) 35,000
(Total) Current Capacity: 35,100 (all seated)
Visiting Supporters' Allocation: 3,450 (in the South Stand)

Club Colours: Red shirts, red shorts
Nearest Railway Station: Middlesbrough
Parking (Car): All parking at stadium is for permit holders
Parking (Coach/Bus): As directed
Police Force and Tel No: Cleveland (01642 248184)
Disabled Visitors' Facilities:
  Wheelchairs: More than 170 places available for disabled fans
  Blind: Commentary available
Anticipated Development(s): There remain long term plans for the ground's capacity to be increased to 42,000 through the construction of extra tiers on the North, South and East stands, although there is no confirmed timetable for this work at the current time.

KEY

C Club Offices
S Club Shop

↑ North direction (approx)

❶ Cargo Fleet Road
❷ To Middlesbrough railway station
❸ To Middlesbrough town centre
❹ Middlesbrough Docks
❺ Shepherdson Way to A66
❻ South Stand
❼ Car parks

Above: 697413; Right: 697417

The season started slowly for Steve McClaren and Boro' as it seemed that the team's European exploits were distracting the squad from the more important task of domestic football and, potentially, securing another stab at the UEFA Cup in 2005/06. As the season progressed, however, Boro' moved up the Premier League table and were ultimately to be guaranteed a UEFA Cup spot again in highly dramatic fashion on the last day of the season. Playing Manchester City, their rivals for the final Cup spot at the City of Manchester Stadium, Boro' needed to avoid defeat to pip the Mancunians to the all-important seventh place. Drawing 1-1 as the game drew to a close, Boro' looked to have sewn up the final spot; however, a late penalty seemed to have changed the balance of fortune — until Robbie Fowler's shot was saved by Mark Schwarzer. Thus Boro' again play in the UEFA Cup — where they progressed to the Quarter Finals in 2004/05 — and can again look optimistically towards finishing in the top seven of the Premier League in the new season. Undoubtedly not strong enough to challenge for a Champions League position, Boro' are now one of the chasing pack.

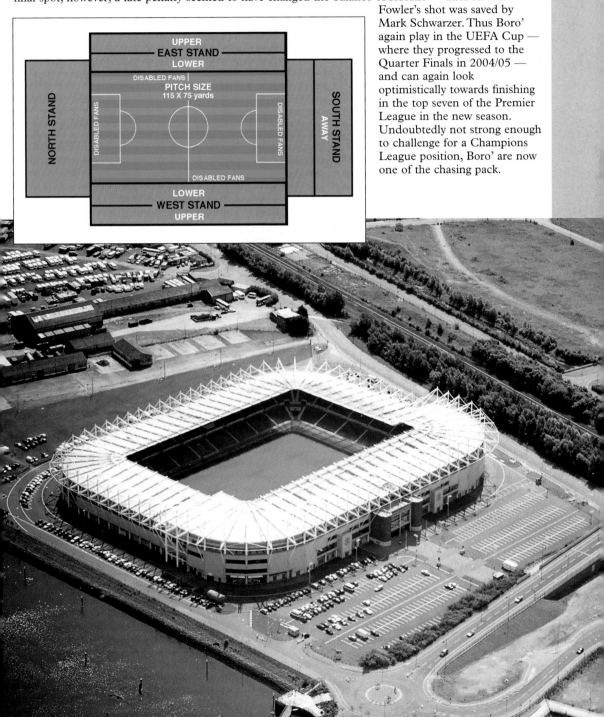

UPPER
EAST STAND
LOWER

NORTH STAND

DISABLED FANS

DISABLED FANS |
PITCH SIZE
115 X 75 yards

DISABLED FANS

SOUTH STAND
AWAY

DISABLED FANS

LOWER
WEST STAND
UPPER

MILLWALL

New Den, Bolina Road, London, SE16 3LN

Tel No: 020 7232 1222
Advance Tickets Tel No: 020 7231 9999
Fax: 020 7231 3663
Web Site: www.millwallfc.premiumtv.co.uk
E-mail: info@millwallplc.com
League: League Championship
Brief History: Founded 1885 as Millwall
Rovers, changed name to Millwall Athletic
(1889) and Millwall (1925). Former Grounds:
Glengall Road, East Ferry Road (2 separate
Grounds), North Greenwich Ground and The
Den – Cold Blow Lane – moved to New Den
1993/94 season. Founder-members Third
Division (1920). Record attendance (at The
Den) 48,672 (at New Den) 20,093

(Total) Current Capacity: 20,150 (all seated)
Visiting Supporters' Allocation: 4,382 in
North Stand
Club Colours: Blue shirts, white shorts
Nearest Railway Station: South Bermondsey
or Surrey Docks (Tube)
Parking (Car): Juno Way car parking (8 mins
walk)
Parking (Coach/Bus): At Ground
Police Force and Tel No: Metropolitan (0207
679 9217)
Disabled Visitors' Facilities:
  Wheelchairs: 200 spaces in West Stand
  Lower Tier
  Blind: Commentary available

KEY

C Club Offices
S Club Shop
E Entrance(s) for visiting
supporters

⬆ North direction (approx)

❶ Bolina Road
❷ To South Bermondsey
station
❸ Footpath to station for away
fans
❹ Zampa Road
❺ Stockholm Road
❻ North Stand (away)

Above: 697379; *Right:* 697384

Following the 2003/04 season, which had seen Millwall reach the FA Cup Final and achieve European football, in many respects 2004/05 was perhaps always destined to be an anticlimax. Never really threatening in the Championship, Dennis Wise's team rarely featured in the push for the Play-Offs either. Off the field, chairman Theo Paphitis announced that he was standing down at the end of the season with Jeff Burnige – who resigned in early July – taking over. Given the close relationship between Paphites and Wise it was always likely that the latter would consider his position as well and it came as little surprise when, after the final match of the season (which saw Millwall draw 0-0 with Burnley to leave the team in 10th position), Wise announced that he was standing down. His successor, Steve Claridge, faces a challenge in making the Lions a serious contender for promotion and so perhaps another season of mid-table obscurity beckons.

MILTON KEYNES DONS

National Hockey Stadium, Silbury Boulevard, Milton Keynes, MK9 1FA

Tel No: 01908 607090
Advance Tickets Tel No: 01908 609000
Fax: 01908 209449
National Hockey Stadium: 01908 246800
Web Site: www.mkdons.premiumtv.co.uk
E-Mail: gemma.jones@mkdons.com
League: League One
Brief History: Founded 1889 at Wimbledon Old Centrals, changed name to Wimbledon in 1905 and to Milton Keynes Dons in 2004. Former grounds: Wimbledon Common, Pepy's Road, Grand Drive, Merton Hall Road, Malden Wanderers Cricket Ground, Plough Lane and moved to Selhurst Park in 1991. Probable move to National Hockey Stadium 2002. Elected to Football League in 1977. Record attendance (Plough Lane) 18,000; (Selhurst Park) 30,115; (National Hockey Stadium) 8,118

(Total) Current Capacity: 9,000 (all seated)
Visiting Supporters' Allocation: 2,300 (West Stand)
Club Colours: White shirts, White shorts
Nearest Railway Station: Milton Keynes Central
Parking (Car): At ground
Parking (Coach/Bus): As directed
Police Force and Tel No: Thames Valley Police (01865 846000)
Disabled Visitors' Facilities:
  Wheelchairs: 48 spaces around the ground
  Blind: No special facility at present
Anticipated Development(s): Work started on the construction of the club's new 30,000-seat capacity stadium in mid-February. The plans anticipate the club relocating from the National Hockey Stadium for the start of the 2006/07 season.

KEY

↑ North direction (approx)

❶ West Stand (away)
❷ To Milton Keynes Central station
❸ Grafton Gate
❹ A509 Portway
❺ A509 Portway to A5 junction
❻ Silbury Boulevard
❼ To town centre

Above: 698885; *Right:* 698894

With the Dons struggling in League one, following relegation at the end of the 2003/04 campaign, Stuart Murdoch parted company with the club in early November after a 4-1 defeat that left the team rooted in the bottom four. Following a period with Jimmy Gilligan as caretaker, which saw the Dons reach the Third Round of the FA Cup, the experienced ex-Bristol city boss, Danny Wilson, took over as manager in early December. Under Wilson the team's form improved and the club looked to be clawing its way out of the relegation zone. The penultimate series of matches, however, saw the Dons drop back into the drop zone and left the club hoping that either Oldham or Torquay would lose and that the Dons could beat high-flying Tranmere at home. In the event, victory over Rovers allied to Torquay's defeat at Colchester meant last day survival for the Dons and League One fare again in 2005/06. However, it's hard to escape the conclusion that Wilson will not face anything other than a struggle against the drop again in the new season.

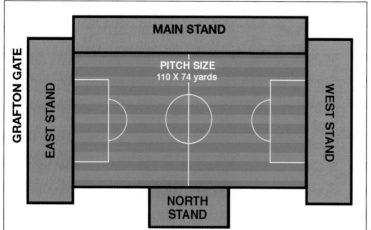

NEWCASTLE UNITED

St. James' Park, Newcastle-upon-Tyne, NE1 4ST

Tel No: 0191 201 8400
Advance Tickets Tel No: 0191 261 1571
Fax: 0191 201 8600
Web Site: www.nufc.premiumtv.co.uk
E-mail: admin@nufc.co.uk
League: F.A. Premier
Brief History: Founded in 1882 as Newcastle East End, changed to Newcastle United in 1892. Former Grounds: Chillingham Road, moved to St. James' Park (former home of defunct Newcastle West End) in 1892. Record attendance 68,386
(Total) Current Capacity: 52,316 (all seated)
Visiting Supporters' Allocation: 3,000 in North West Stand
Club Colours: Black and white striped shirts, black shorts

Nearest Railway Station: Newcastle Central
Parking (Car): Leazes car park and street parking
Parking (Coach/Bus): Leazes car park
Police Force and Tel No: Northumbria (0191 232 3451)
Disabled Visitors' Facilities:
  Wheelchairs: 103 spaces available
  Blind: Commentary available
Anticipated Development(s): With work now completed on both the enlarged Millburn and Sir John Hall stands, the capacity at St James' Park is now about 52,000. Further redevelopment at the ground is, however, problematic given the lie of the land on the north side, and the club has no immediate plans for further work once the current programme is completed.

KEY
C Club Offices
S Club Shop

↑ North direction (approx)

❶ St. James's Park
❷ Strawberry Place
❸ Gallowgate
❹ Away Section
❺ To Newcastle Central BR Station (¹/₂ mile) & A6127(M)
❻ Car Park
❼ Barrack Road (A189)
❽ To A1 and North
❾ Corporation Street
❿ Percy Road
⓫ Metro Station

Above: 694859; Right: 694852

Sentiment counts for little in the modern game and, even before the season started, Newcastle chairman Freddie Shepherd announced that Sir Bobby Robson's contract would not be renewed at the end of 2004/05. In the event, despite the signing of several high profile players, such as the Dutchman Patrick Kluivert, a poor start to the season — two points out of the first four games — cost Sir Bobby his job at the August Bank holiday. Although the pundits favoured figures such as Steve Bruce and David O'Leary, the club appointed ex-Blackburn supremo Graeme Souness to fill Robson's position. Thereafter the club had something of a roller-coaster ride, stringing together some excellent results but, ultimately, failing to progress beyond the quarter finals of the UEFA Cup — losing tamely to Sporting Lisbon despite the benefit of a 1-0 home win and an away goal — and the semi-finals of the FA Cup — losing abjectly to Manchester United 4-1. Troubles on the field were compounded by internecine strife between the players, marked by the unseemly spectacle of Kieron Dyer and Lee Bowyer fighting each other during the home game against Aston Villa. No doubt the close season will see significant changes in the playing personnel at St James's Park as Souness imposes his authority. The one positive is perhaps the fact that Alan Shearer has confirmed that he will play one further season. Much will depend on Souness's transfer dealings during the summer, but it's hard to escape the conclusion that the Premier League title will not be coming to Tyneside and that the club's best hopes of silverware will again come in cup competitions.

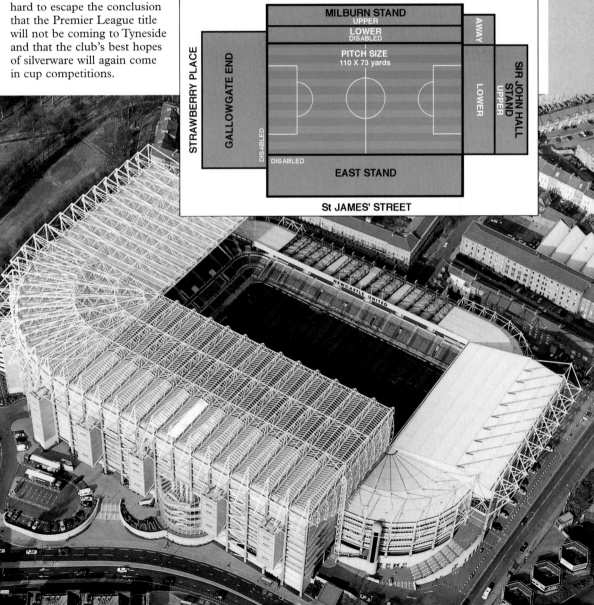

NORTHAMPTON TOWN

Sixfields Stadium, Northampton, NN5 5QA

Tel No: 01604 757773
Advance Tickets Tel No: 01604 588338
Fax: 01604 751613
Web Site: www.ntfc.premiumtv.co.uk
E-Mail: secretary@ntfc.tv
League: League Two
Brief History: Founded 1897. Former, County, Ground was part of Northamptonshire County Cricket Ground. Moved to Sixfields Stadium during early 1994/95 season. Record attendance 24,523 (at County Ground); 7,557 (at Sixfields)
(Total) Current Capacity: 7,653 (all seated)
Visiting Supporters' Allocation: 850 (in South Stand; can be increased to 1,150 if necessary)

Club Colours: Claret with white sleeved shirts, white shorts
Nearest Railway Station: Northampton
Parking (Car): Adjacent to Ground
Parking (Coach/Bus): Adjacent to Ground
Police Force and Tel No: Northants (01604 700700)
Disabled Visitors' Facilities:
Wheelchairs: Available on all four sides
Blind: Available
Anticipated Development(s): The club has plans to increase the capacity of the Sixfields stadium to c16,000 all-seated although there is no timescale for this work.

KEY
C Club Offices
S Club Shop
E Entrance(s) for visiting supporters
R Refreshment bars for visiting supporters
T Toilets for visiting supporters

⬆ North direction (approx)

❶ South Stand (away)
❷ Athletics Stand
❸ Upton Way
❹ Car parks
❺ A45 towards A43 (Towcester and A5)
❻ Weedon Road
❼ To Town Centre and station
❽ A45 to M1 (Jct 16)

Above: 696943; Right: 696943

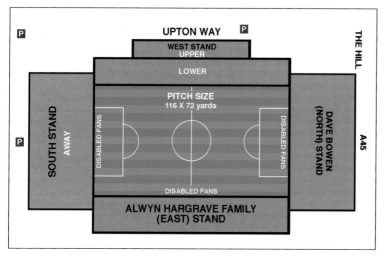

Diagram labels:
- UPTON WAY
- P (parking, left and right)
- WEST STAND UPPER
- LOWER
- PITCH SIZE 116 X 72 yards
- SOUTH STAND
- AWAY
- DISABLED FANS
- DISABLED FANS
- DISABLED FANS
- DAVE BOWEN (NORTH) STAND
- THE HILL
- A45
- ALWYN HARGRAVE FAMILY (EAST) STAND

Another season of some disappointment for Colin Calderwood and Northampton Town saw the club, widely seen as one of the pre-season favourites for promotion, fail to sustain a meaningful challenge and being forced, yet again, into the Play-Offs, by finishing in sixth position. Having lost in the semi-finals to Mansfield in 2003/04, there was every hope that the Cobblers could do better in 2004/05. In the event, however, the club was to lose to Lincoln City and therefore another season of League Two fare beckons for the Sixfields' faithful. One factor in the club's failure in 2004/05 was a series of mid-season injuries; provided that Calderwood can call on a fit squad in 2005/06 then again the team should be able to mount a serious challenge for promotion.

NORWICH CITY

Carrow Road, Norwich, NR1 1JE

Tel No: 01603 760760
Advance Tickets Tel No: 0870 444 1902
Fax: 01603 613886
Web Site: www.canaries.premiumtv.co.uk
E-Mail: reception@ncfc-canaries.co.uk
League: League Championship
Brief History: Founded 1902. Former grounds: Newmarket Road and the Nest, Rosary Road; moved to Carrow Road in 1935. Founder-members 3rd Division (1920). Record attendance 43,984
(Total) Current Capacity: 26,034
Visiting Supporters' Allocation: 2,500 maximum in South Stand
Club Colours: Yellow with green side panel shirts, green shorts
Nearest Railway Station: Norwich
Parking (Car): City centre car parks

Parking (Coach/Bus): Lower Clarence Road
Police Force and Tel No: Norfolk (01603 768769)
Disabled Visitors' Facilities:
  Wheelchairs: New facility in corner infill stand
  Blind: Commentary available
Anticipated Development(s): The £3 million corner infill between the new Jarrold (South) Stand and the River End was opened in two stages in early 2005. The upper tier provides seats for 850 and the lower for 660. There is also a new disabled area located between the two tiers. This work takes Carrow Road's capacity to 26,000. As part of the plans for the Jarrold Stand, the pitch was relocated one metre away from the City Stand; this will facilitate the construction of a second tier on the City Stand in the future if required.

KEY

C Club Offices
S Club Shop

↑ North direction (approx)

❶ Carrow Road
❷ A47 King Street
❸ River Wensum
❹ Riverside
❺ Car Park
❻ Norwich BR Station
❼ South Stand
❽ Geoffrey Watling (City) Stand
❾ Barclay End Stand
❿ The Norwich & Peterborough (River End) Stand

Above: 698898; Right: 698903

Promoted at the end of the 2003/04 season, the Canaries were always going to be one of the pre-season favourites for an automatic return to the League Championship but it was tense battle all the way to the end for Nigel Worthington and his team. A slow start and a tendency to leak goals in a major way undermined the club's efforts to stay in the Premier League but the occasional great result, such as defeating Manchester United at Carrow Road, ensured that judgement day was delayed until the final Sunday of the season — the first time in Premier League history when no single club had already been relegated by this stage of the season. Any one of four clubs could have survived but Norwich at the start of the day were in the all important 17th position — better their opponents' results and survival was assured. An away fixture at Craven Cottage was the team's last match; Fulham had struggled all season but Norwich had not won away from Carrow Road all season. The result? A 6-0 drubbing for Norwich and relegation to the Championship. Next season, Delia can be shouting 'Let's be having you' to the likes of Luton Town and Hull City. However, Norwich's sojourn in the Premier League was well structured and the squad should be well capable of maintaining a challenge to make an immediate return.

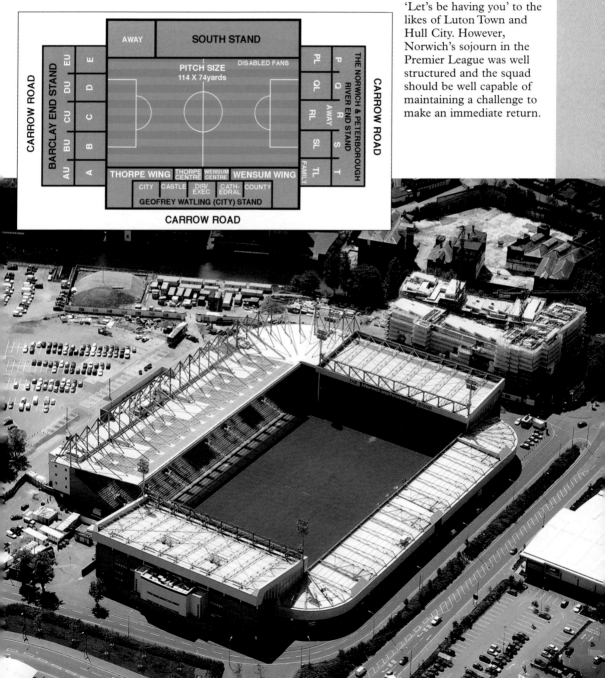

NOTTINGHAM FOREST

City Ground, Nottingham, NG2 5FJ

Tel No: 0115 982 4444
Advance Tickets Tel No: 0871 226 1980
Fax: 0115 982 4455
Web Site: www.nottinghamforest.premiumtv.co.uk
E-Mail: enquiries@nottinghamforest.co.uk
League: League One
Brief History: Founded 1865 as Forest Football Club, changed name to Nottingham Forest (c1879). Former Grounds: Forest Recreation Ground, Meadow Cricket Ground, Trent Bridge (Cricket Ground), Parkside, Gregory Ground and Town Ground, moved to City Ground in 1898. Founder-members of Second Division (1892). Record attendance 49,945
(Total) Current Capacity: 30,602 (all seated)
Visiting Supporters' Allocation: Approx 4,750

Club Colours: Red shirts, white shorts
Nearest Railway Station: Nottingham
Parking (Car): East car park and street parking
Parking (Coach/Bus): East car park
Police Force and Tel No: Nottinghamshire (0115 948 1888)
Disabled Visitors' Facilities:
  Wheelchairs: Front of Brian Clough Stand
  Blind: No special facility
Anticipated Development(s): The club has long-term plans for the redevelopment of the Main Stand, with a view to increasing the ground's capacity to 40,000, but nothing will happen until the club reclaims a position in the Premiership.

KEY

C Club Offices
S Club Shop
E Entrance(s) for visiting supporters

↑ North direction (approx)

❶ Radcliffe Road
❷ Lady Bay Bridge Road
❸ Trent Bridge
❹ Trent Bridge Cricket Ground
❺ Bridgford Stand
❻ River Trent
❼ Nottingham Midland BR Station (½ mile)

Above: 698938; *Right:* 698930

If a week is a long time in politics, a year must be eternity in football. In the autumn of 2003 Joe Kinnear was brought into manage Forest and, under his stewardship, the club managed to escape the drop. However, in 2004/05 the team again struggled and, in the middle of December, following a 3-0 defeat at local rivals Derby County that left Forest in the drop zone, Kinnear resigned, with Mick Harford taking temporary charge of the team. In early January, following the club's victory in the 3rd round of the FA Cup, ex-West Brom boss Gary Megson took over. However, despite Megson's efforts, the club failed to escape from the drop and so Forest now face League One football in 2005/06. Long gone are the heady days when the club won the European Cup on two occasions; indeed, Forest represent the only team to have won the competition now to be playing in their home country's third tier of football. The club does have a strong fan base and, in Megson, an astute manager. As a result, Forest should undoubtedly be challenging for promotion although the lesson of the other ex-Premiership teams in the division – Barnsley, Bradford City, Oldham and Swindon — is not an encouraging one.

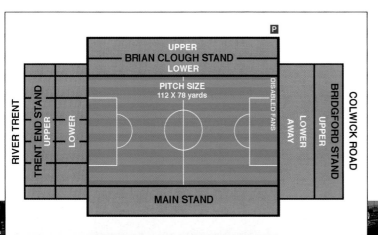

NOTTS COUNTY

Meadow Lane, Nottingham, NG2 3HJ

Tel No: 0115 952 9000
Advance Tickets Tel No: 0115 955 7204
Fax: 0115 955 3994
Web Site: www.nottscountyfc.premiumtv.co.uk
E-Mail: info@nottscountyfc.co.uk
League: League Two
Brief History: Founded 1862 (oldest club in Football League) as Nottingham, changed to Notts County in c1882. Former Grounds: Notts Cricket Ground (Beeston), Castle Cricket Ground, Trent Bridge Cricket Ground, moved to Meadow Lane in 1910. Founder-members Football League (1888). Record attendance 47,310

(Total) Current Capacity: 19,600 (seated)
Visiting Supporters' Allocation: 5,438 (seated)
Club Colours: Black and white striped shirts, black shorts
Nearest Railway Station: Nottingham Midland
Parking (Car): Mainly street parking
Parking (Coach/Bus): Cattle market
Police Force and Tel No: Nottingham (0115 948 1888)
Disabled Visitors' Facilities:
Wheelchairs: Meadow Lane/Jimmy Sirrel/Derek Pavis Stands
Blind: No special facility

KEY

E Entrance(s) for visiting supporters

R Refreshment bars for visiting supporters

T Toilets for visiting supporters

↑ North direction (approx)

❶ A6011 Meadow Lane
❷ County Road
❸ A60 London Road
❹ River Trent
❺ Nottingham Midland BR Station (½ mile)
❻ Jimmy Sirrel Stand
❼ Kop Stand (away)
❽ Derek Pavis Stand
❾ Family (Meadow Lane) Stand

Above: 698926; *Right:* 698913

After a disappointing start to the season, culminating in a 5-1 rout by Rushden & Diamonds which left the Magpies just above the League Two drop zone, Gary Mills was sacked as Manager at the start of November. Ian Richardson took over as caretaker player-manager and, following a series of good results, the club dragged itself away from the drop zone. As a result, Richardson was confirmed in his position until the end of the season. Away from the league, County had some success in the cup competitions defeating Bradford City at Valley Parade and Swindon Town at home in the Carling Cup and FA Cup respectively. In Mid-April it was announced that Richardson would not continue in the role and ex-Stoke boss Gudjon Thordarsson was appointed to take over for the 2005/06 campaign. However, it's difficult to escape the view that County will continue to struggle in League Two and that another battle against relegation beckons.

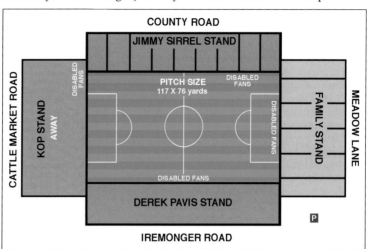

OLDHAM ATHLETIC

Boundary Park, Oldham, OL1 2PA

Tel No: 0871 226 2235
Advance Tickets Tel No: 0871 226 2235
Fax: 0871 226 1715
Web Site: www.oldhamathletic.premiumtv.co.uk
E-Mail: tickets@oldhamathletic.co.uk
League: League One
Brief History: Founded 1897 as Pine Villa, changed name to Oldham Athletic in 1899. Former Grounds: Berry's Field, Pine Mill, Athletic Ground (later named Boundary Park), Hudson Fold, moved to Boundary Park in 1906. Record attendance 47,671.
(Total) Current Capacity: 13,624 (all seated)
Visiting Supporters' Allocation: 1,800 minimum, 4,600 maximum
Club Colours: Blue shirts, blue shorts
Nearest Railway Station: Oldham Werneth
Parking (Car): Lookers Stand car park
Parking (Coach/Bus): At Ground
Other Clubs Sharing Ground: Oldham Roughyeads RLFC
Police Force and Tel No: Greater Manchester (0161 624 0444)
Disabled Visitors' Facilities:
  Wheelchairs: Rochdale Road and Seton Stands
  Blind: No special facility
Anticipated Development(s): The plans for the construction of a new 15,000-seat ground at Clayton Playing Fields in conjunction with the local RLFC club have been abandoned. As a result, Athletic will now seek to redevelop Boundary Park further, with the first phase being the construction of a new two-tier stand, costing £15 million, to replace the Lookers Stand. There is, however, no confirmed timetable for this work at the current time.

KEY

C Club Offices
E Entrance(s) for visiting supporters

↑ North direction (approx)

❶ A663 Broadway
❷ Furtherwood Road
❸ Chadderton Way
❹ To A627(M) and M62
❺ To Oldham Werneth BR Station (1½ miles)
❻ Car Park
❼ Rochdale Road Stand (away)
❽ SSL Stand
❾ Lookers Stand
❿ Pukka Pies Stand

122

Above: 697199; *Right:* 697195

At the end of February, with the Latics having been defeated in the team's last seven league matches, culminating in a 5-1 reverse at Bristol City, Brian Talbot departed the Boundary Park managerial hot seat after almost a year in charge. He was replaced by Tony Philliskirk as caretaker but the club moved quickly to appoint ex-Rotherham boss Ronnie Moore as manager until the end of the season. Under Moore the club's form improved, particularly as a result of the scoring prowess of on-loan Luke Beckett, but League One safety was not assured until the final Saturday of the season. One of three teams — Athletic, Milton Keynes Dons or Torquay — faced the drop. However, a 2-1 victory over Bradford City ensured that Oldham survived and that Torquay lost out. The season was not wholly disastrous — the club did defeat Manchester City 1-0 in the FA Cup — but the team's league form was the cause of Talbot's departure.

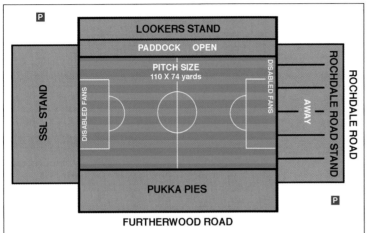

OXFORD UNITED

Kassam Stadium, Grenoble Road, Blackbird Leys, Oxford OX4 4XP

Tel No: 01865 337500
Advance Tickets Tel No: 01865 337533
Fax: 01865 337555
Web Site: www.oufc.premiumtv.co.uk
E-Mail: admin@oufc.co.uk
League: League Two
Brief History: Founded in 1893 as Headington (later Headington United), changed name to Oxford United in 1960. Former grounds: Britannia Inn Field, Headington Quarry, Wooten's Field, Manor Ground and The Paddocks. The club moved back to the Manor Ground in 1925. Moved — finally — to new ground at Minchery Farm in 2001. Record attendance (at the Manor Ground) 22,730.
(Total) Current Capacity: 12,500
Visiting Supporters' Allocation: c5,000 maximum in North Stand

Club Colours: Yellow with blue trim shirts and navy with yellow trim shorts
Nearest Railway Station: Oxford
Parking (Car): 1,100 spaces at ground
Parking (Coach/Bus): As directed
Police Force and Tel No: Thames Valley (01865 777501)
Disabled Visitors' Facilities:
  Wheelchairs: c80 disabled spaces
  Blind: No special facility
Anticipated Development(s): Although the club has plans for the construction of the fourth side of the ground there is no confirmed timescale as to when this work will be undertaken.

KEY
C Club Offices
E Entrance(s) for visiting supporters

↑ North direction (approx)

❶ Grenoble Road
❷ To A4074
❸ Northfield School
❹ To Oxford city centre and railway station (four/five miles respectively)
❺ Blackbird Leys Estate
❻ Knights Road
❼ North Stand
❽ South Stand
❾ East Stand
❿ To B480

Above: 699124; *Right:* 699129

With United hovering just above the League Two drop zone and having been knocked out of the FA Cup in the First Round at Rochdale, Graham Rix was relieved of the manager's job and moved upstairs, to be replaced by youth team coach, Darren Patterson. In early December, chairman Firoz Kassam announced that ex-Argentinian international Ramon Diaz, 'a friend of a friend', had agreed to take over for six months in the hope of keeping United out of the drop zone. Under the new management, United drew away from the relegation battle and ultimately finished in 15th position. However, in early May it was announced that the club and Diaz had failed to agree upon the terms of a new contract and that Diaz had left the club, along with his backroom staff, to return to Argentina. Kassam moved swiftly to appoint the experienced Brian Talbot as manager. Talbot's experience in managing clubs at this level should ensure that the new season is more successful at the Kassam Stadium and United should certainly have the potential to make the Play-Offs in 2005/06

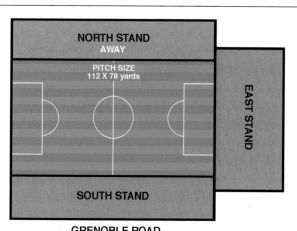

NORTH STAND
AWAY

PITCH SIZE
112 X 78 yards

EAST STAND

SOUTH STAND

GRENOBLE ROAD

PETERBOROUGH UNITED

London Road, Peterborough, Cambs, PE2 8AL

Tel No: 01733 563947
Advance Tickets Tel No: 01753 563947
Fax: 01733 344140
Web Site: www.theposh.premiumtv.co.uk
E-Mail: info@theposh.com
League: League Two
Brief History: Founded in 1934 (no connection with former 'Peterborough and Fletton United' FC). Elected to Football League in 1960. Record attendance 30,096
(Total) Current Capacity: 15,314 (7,669 seated)
Visiting Supporters' Allocation: 4,758 (756 seated)
Club Colours: Blue shirts, white shorts

Nearest Railway Station: Peterborough
Parking (Car): Peterborough
Parking (Coach/Bus): At ground
Police Force and Tel No: Cambridgeshire (01733 563232)
Disabled Visitors' Facilities:
  Wheelchairs: South Stand
  Blind: No special facility
Future Development(s): Following the reroofing of the Moys and London Road ends, long term plans exist for the construction of a new Main Stand — for which plans have been prepared — and other work. However, there is no confirmed timetable for this at present.

KEY

C	Club Offices
S	Club Shop
E	Entrance(s) for visiting supporters
R	Refreshment bars for visiting supporters
T	Toilets for visiting supporters

⬆ North direction (approx)

❶ A15 London Road
❷ Car Parks
❸ Peterborough BR Station (1 mile)
❹ Glebe Road
❺ A605
❻ To A1 (north) (5 miles)
❼ River Nene
❽ To Whittlesey
❾ To A1 (south) (5 miles)
❿ Thomas Cook Stand
⓫ London Road Terrace
⓬ Moys Terrace (away)
⓭ Main Stand

Above: 697321; *Right:* 697312

Towards the end of March, Barry Fry announced that the stress of being both club owner and manager was not one that he wished to continue into the new campaign. Not only was it a struggle off the field for Fry, it was also a battle on the field for his Posh team as the squad battled to retain the club's League One status. In the end, however, the team's five-year stint at this level came to an end as the team finished a disappointing 23rd some 12 points off safety. For the future, much will depend on the new manager — Mark Wright — and whether he is able to turn things around quickly. As with other relegated teams, Posh will be fancying their chances of making an immediate return to the higher level and certainly a Play-Off looks a reasonable likelihood.

GLEBE ROAD

THOMAS COOK SOUTH STAND
UPPER

DISABLED (D-WING)

LOWER

PITCH SIZE
112 X 71 yards

MOYS TERRACE (COVERED) AWAY

LONDON ROAD TERRACE (COVERED)

LONDON ROAD

ENCLOSURE

DISABLED

A STAND AWAY

MAIN STAND

WEST WING

PLYMOUTH ARGYLE

Home Park, Plymouth, PL2 3DQ

Tel No: 01752 562561
Advance Tickets Tel No: 0871 222 1288
Fax: 01752 606167
Web-site: www.pafc.premiumtv.co.uk
E-mail: argyle@pafc.co.uk
League: League Championship
Brief History: Founded 1886 as Argyle Athletic Club, changed name to Plymouth Argyle in 1903. Founder-members Third Division (1920). Record attendance 43,596
(Total) Current Capacity: 20,134 (15,684 seated)
Visiting Supporters' Allocation: 1,300 (all seated) in Barn Park End Stand up to maximum of 2,000
Club Colours: White and green shirts, green shorts

Nearest Railway Station: Plymouth
Parking (Car): Car park adjacent
Parking (Coach/Bus): Central car park
Police Force and Tel No: Devon & Cornwall (0990 777444)
Disabled Visitors' Facilities:
  Wheelchairs: Devonport End
  Blind: Commentary available
Anticipated Development(s): Work on the three new stands at Home Park progressed well, with work being completed during the 2001/02 season. Plans, however, for the demolition of the existing Main Stand and its replacement have been resurrected as part of a £37 million redevelopment. If work progresses the new stand would be completed in 2006.

KEY
C Club Offices
S Club Shop

↑ North direction (approx)

❶ A386 Outland Road
❷ Car Park
❸ Devonport Road
❹ Central Park
❺ Town Centre & Plymouth BR Station (¹/₂ mile)
❻ To A38 (½ mile)

128

Above: 692218; Right: 692209

Promoted from League One at the end of the 2003/04 season, the primary aim for Plymouth was for the club to secure its League Championship status and, although the club hovered dangerously close to the drop zone at times, relegation was probably never a serious threat — particularly given the weakness of both Rotherham and Nottingham Forest — and finishing in 17th place, three points above relegated Gillingham, was perhaps as good as it could be. Provided that manager Bobby Williamson is able to strengthen his squad during the close season, then the team should certainly be able to safeguard its League Championship status again and, perhaps, move into the top half of the division. Away from the League, the team suffered the embarrassment of a 3-2 defeat away at Yeovil of League Two in the first round of the Carling Cup, at which time Argyle were riding high in a slightly false second place in the Championship.

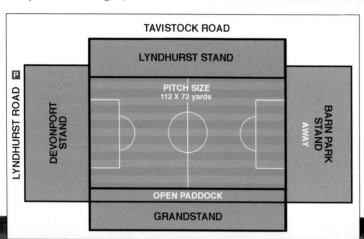

PORTSMOUTH

Fratton Park, 57 Frogmore Road, Portsmouth, Hants, PO4 8RA

Tel No: 02392 731204
Advance Tickets Tel No: 0871 230 1898
Fax: 02392 734129
Web Site: www.pompeyfc.premiumtv.co.uk
E-Mail: info@pompeyfc.co.uk
League: F.A. Premier
Brief History: Founded 1898. Founder-
members Third Division (1920). Record
attendance 51,385
(Total) Current Capacity: 20,101 (all seated)
  Visiting Supporters' Allocation: 3,121
  (max) in Milton Stand
Club Colours: Blue shirts, white shorts
Nearest Railway Station: Fratton
Parking (Car): Street parking
Parking (Coach/Bus): As directed by Police
Police Force and Tel No: Hampshire (02392
  321111)

Disabled Visitors' Facilities:
  Wheelchairs: TY Europe Stand
  Blind: No special facility
Anticipated Development(s): The club was
  given formal approval by the local authority for
  the construction of the new ground in late July
  2004. The proposed realignment of the ground
  will have an initial capacity of 28,000 rising to
  36,000 if required. The scheme is scheduled to
  cost £25 million and will be undertaken by
  Barr Construction. Work was scheduled to
  start in November 2005 with the pitch being
  rotated at the end of the 2005/06 season but
  demolition of the North Stand will now take
  place at the end of the season. Apart from a
  new North Stand, work also is planned to
  include new West and East stands with part of
  the Leitch-designed South Stand being retained.

KEY
C Club Offices
S Club Shop
E Entrance(s) for visiting
supporters
R Refreshment bars for visiting
supporters
T Toilets for visiting supporters

⬆ North direction (approx)

❶ Alverstone Road
❷ Carisbrook Road
❸ A288 Milton Road
❹ A2030 Velder Avenue A27
❺ A2030 Goldsmith Avenue
❻ Fratton BR station (1/2 mile)
❼ TY Europe Stand
❽ Milton End
❾ North Stand
❿ South Stand

Above: 699188; *Right:* 699192

Towards the end of November, the rumbling dispute between Milan Mandaric and Harry Redknapp erupted again with the chairman imposing a Director of Football, Velimer Zajec, on the manager. As a result both Redknapp and his assistant Jim Smith resigned, leaving Zajec to take temporary charge of the team with Joe Jordan as his assistant. The club's first result under the new boss was a 2-0 victory at Bolton, Pompey's first away win of the season. Although the club's initial performances improved — with eight points being amassed from the first five games — it was always likely that the club would bring in an experienced manager from outside, particularly as later results worsened. Following a defeat at Fulham, which left Pompey just above the drop zone, it was confirmed in early April that ex-Marseille boss Alain Perrin, assisted by David Pleat in a consultancy role until the end of the season, would take over, having accepted a two-year contract from Milan Mandaric. Under Perrin, Pompey secured their Premier League status by finishing in 16th place some six points above relegated Norwich and Crystal Palace and local pride was no doubt satisfied as defeat away at West Brom on the final Sunday of the season was one factor in sending Southampton into the League Championship.

However, with several experienced players moving on during the summer, Perrin will have a difficult task ensuring sufficient quality at Fratton Park if 2005/06 isn't to turn out to be a battle against following Saints into the Championship.

MILTON LANE

UPPER
NORTH STAND
LOWER

PITCH SIZE
114 X 72 yards

FROGMORE ROAD

TY EUROPE STAND

DISABLED FANS

INTER-CITY CASH
(MILTON) END
AWAY

ASPLEY ROAD

SOUTH STAND

CARISBROOKE ROAD

PORT VALE

Vale Park, Burslem, Stoke-on-Trent, ST6 1AW

Tel No: 01782 655800
Advance Tickets Tel No: 01782 811707
Fax: 01782 836875
Web Site: www.port-vale.premiumtv.co.uk
E-Mail: pvfc@port-vale.co.uk
League: League One
Brief History: Founded 1876 as Burslem Port Vale, changed name to 'Port Vale' in 1907 (reformed club). Former Grounds: The Meadows Longport, Moorland Road Athletic Ground, Cobridge Athletic Grounds, Recreation Ground Hanley, moved to Vale Park in 1950. Founder-members Second Division (1892). Record attendance 48,749
(Total) Current Capacity: 22,356 (all seated)
Visiting Supporters' Allocation: 4,550 (in Hamil Road [Phones4U] Stand)

Club Colours: White shirts, black shorts
Nearest Railway Station: Longport (two miles)
Parking (Car): Car park at Ground
Parking (Coach/Bus): Hamil Road car park
Police Force and Tel No: Staffordshire (01782 577114)
Disabled Visitors' Facilities:
  Wheelchairs: 20 spaces in new Britannic Disabled Stand
  Blind: Commentary available
Anticipated Development(s): After some years of standing half completed, the club's new owners completed the roof over the Lorne Street Stand during the 2004/05 season although as can be seen in the accompanying photographs, fitting out remains to be completed.

KEY

E Entrance(s) for visiting supporters

⬆ North direction (approx)

❶ Car Parks
❷ Hamil Road
❸ Lorne Street
❹ To B5051 Moorland Road
❺ To Burslem Town Centre
❻ Railway Stand
❼ Sentinel Stand
❽ Hamil Road Stand
❾ Lorne Street Stand
❿ Family Section

Above: 698939; *Right:* 698947

A hugely disappointing season at Vale Park in 2004/05 after Martin Foyle's team had just failed to make the Play-Offs at the end of 2003/04. Finishing in 18th place, five points off the drop zone, can be explained by the fact that the club struggled to score goals all season, the total of 49 being the lowest of any team other than relegated Stockport and Peterborough (both of whom scored 49 times as well) in the division, a fact no doubt caused by the loss of Steve McPhee and Steve Booker before and during the season. Unless Foyle is successful in significantly strengthening the squad during the close season, it's hard to escape the conclusion that 2005/06 will again be a battle to stay clear of the relegation zone.

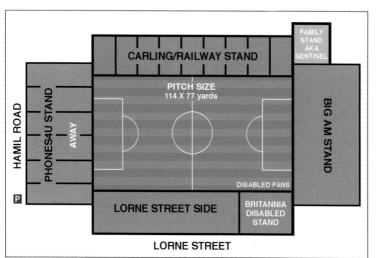

HAMIL ROAD

PHONES4U STAND

AWAY

CARLING/RAILWAY STAND

PITCH SIZE
114 X 77 yards

FAMILY
STAND
AKA
SENTINEL

BIG AM STAND

DISABLED FANS

LORNE STREET SIDE

BRITANNIA
DISABLED
STAND

LORNE STREET

P

PRESTON NORTH END

Deepdale, Sir Tom Finney Way, Preston, PR1 6RU

Tel No: 0870 442 1964
Advance Tickets Tel No: 0870 4421966
Fax: 01772 693366
Web Site: www.pnefc.premiumtv.co.uk
E-Mail: enquiries@pne.com
League: League Championship
Brief History: Founded 1867 as a Rugby Club, changed to soccer in 1881. Former ground: Moor Park, moved to (later named) Deepdale in 1875. Founder-members Football League (1888). Record attendance 42,684
(Total) Current Capacity: 22,225 (all seated)
Visiting Supporters' Allocation: 6,000 maximum in Bill Shankly Stand
Club Colours: White shirts, blue shorts
Nearest Railway Station: Preston (2 miles)
Parking (Car): West Stand car park

Parking (Coach/Bus): West Stand car park
Police Force and Tel No: Lancashire (01772 203203)
Disabled Visitors' Facilities:
  Wheelchairs: Tom Finney Stand and Bill Shankly Stand
  Blind: Earphones Commentary
Anticipated Development(s): The completion of the £3 million 6,100-seat Alan Kelly (Town End) Stand means that Deepdale has now been completely rebuilt on three sides. Planning permission has been granted for the construction of the construction of a new two-tier stand to replace the existing Pavilion Stand, taking the ground's capacity to 30,000. However, there is no confirmed timescale for the work at the present time.

KEY

S Club Shop

↑ North direction (approx)

❶ A6033 Deepdale Road
❷ Lawthorpe Road
❸ Car Park
❹ A5085 Blackpool Road
❺ Preston BR Station (2 miles)
❻ Bill Shankly Stand
❼ Tom Finney Stand
❽ Town End Stand

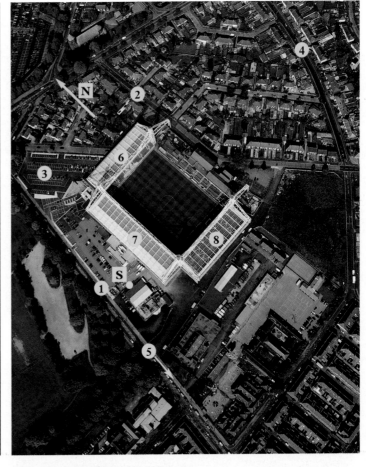

Above: 699138; *Right:* 699139

Following a dismal start to the season, it was announced at the August Bank Holiday that Craig Brown, the ex-boss of Scotland, had parted with Preston 'by mutual consent'. Billy Davies, sometime manager of Motherwell, took over as caretaker, with the board suggesting that he had the opportunity, by the end of September, to make the full-time post his. Following four wins in six games, the team had climbed to 11th in the division with the result that Davies was confirmed as new manager towards the end of September. Under Davis the team prospered and, despite a last day defeat at rivals Derby County, were confirmed in the Play-Offs where, ironically, they faced Derby again. Victory 2-0 at home combined with a 0-0 draw at Pride Park was sufficient to send North End to the final against West Ham. Unfortunately, however, despite having defeated the Hammers twice in the Championship during 2004/05, a third defeat proved one game too many and North End were ultimately defeated 1-0 with a Bobby Zamora strike proving decisive. Nonetheless, a good foundation has been laid for the 2005/06 season and the club certainly now has the potential to reclaim a top-flight place for the first time in 45 years.

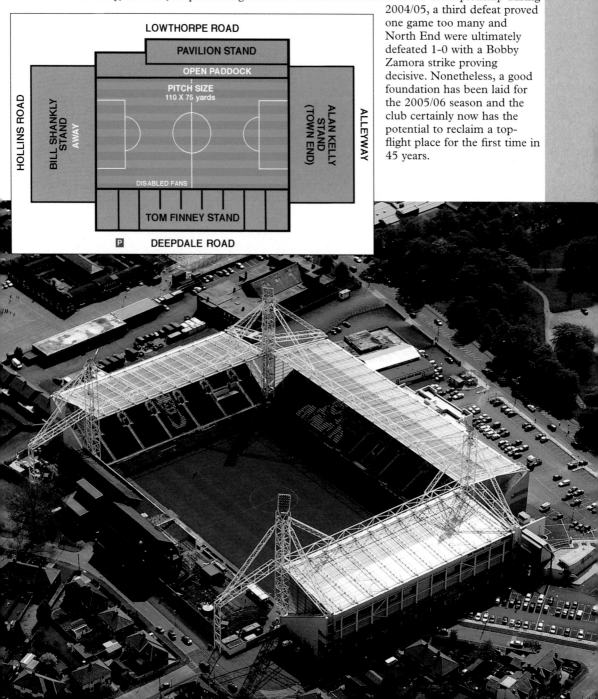

QUEENS PARK RANGERS

Loftus Road Stadium, South Africa Road, London, W12 7PA

Tel No: 020 8743 0262
Advance Tickets Tel No: 0870 112 1967
Fax: 020 8749 0994
Web Site: www.qpr.premiumtv.co.uk
League: League Championship
Brief History: Founded 1885 as 'St. Jude's Institute', amalgamated with Christchurch Rangers to become Queens Park Rangers in 1886. Football League record number of former Grounds and Ground moves (13 different venues, 17 changes), including White City Stadium (twice) final move to Loftus Road in 1963. Founder-members Third Division (1920). Record attendance (at Loftus Road) 35,353
(Total) Current Capacity: 19,148 (all seated)
Visiting Supporters' Allocation: 2,500 (maximum)

Club Colours: Blue and white hooped shirts, white shorts
Nearest Railway Station: Shepherds Bush and White City (both tube)
Parking (Car): White City NCP and street parking
Parking (Coach/Bus): White City NCP
Police Force and Tel No: Metropolitan (020 8741 6212)
Disabled Visitors' Facilities:
  Wheelchairs: Ellerslie Road Stand and West Paddock
  Blind: Ellerslie Road Stand
Anticipated Development(s): There is vague talk of possible relocation, but nothing has been confirmed. Given the constrained site occupied by Loftus Road, it will be difficult to increase the existing ground's capacity.

KEY

C Club Offices
S Club Shop
E Entrance(s) for visiting supporters

↑ North direction (approx)

❶ South Africa Road
❷ To White City Tube Station, A219 Wood Lane and A40 Western Avenue
❸ A4020 Uxbridge Road
❹ To Shepherds Bush Tube Station
❺ To Acton Central Station
❻ BBC Television Centre
❼ Loftus Road
❽ Bloemfontein Road

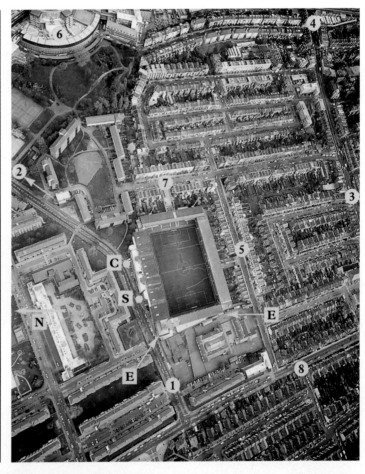

Above: 695957; Right: 695948

Following promotion at the end of the 2003/04 season, many expected Ian Holloway's team to struggle to consolidate in the League Championship but the team prospered and, in finishing in 11th position some 11 points off the Play-Offs, the team has laid the foundations for a further season in the League Championship in 2005/06. Given the potential strength of the three teams relegated from the Premier League — all are better placed to make an immediate return to the top flight in financial terms than the teams relegated in 2003/04, QPR may well struggle to achieve anything better than a Play-Off place, but at least the club's League Championship status looks secure.

SOUTH AFRICA ROAD

SOUTH AFRICA ROAD STAND

SEATED/COVERED PADDOCK

DISABLED FANS PITCH SIZE
112 X 72 yards

DISABLED FANS

ELLERSLIE ROAD STAND

ELLERSLIE ROAD

BLOEMFONTEIN ROAD

SCHOOL END

AWAY

LOWER

UPPER

LOFTUS ROAD STAND

LOFTUS ROAD

READING

Madejski Stadium, Bennet Road, Reading, RG2 0FL

Tel No: 0118 968 1100
Advance Tickets Tel No: 0118 968 1000
Fax: 0118 968 1101
Web Site: www.readingfc.premiumtv.co.uk
E-Mail: customerservice@readingfc.co.uk
League: League Championship
Brief History: Founded 1871. Amalgamated with Reading Hornets in 1877 and with Earley in 1889. Former Grounds: Reading Recreation Ground, Reading Cricket Ground, Coley Park, Caversham Cricket Cround and Elm Park (1895-1998); moved to the Madejski Stadium at the start of the 1998/99 season. Founder-members of the Third Division in 1920. Record attendance (at Elm Park) 33,042; (at Madejski Stadium) 22,034
(Total) Current Capacity: 24,200 (all seated)
Visiting Supporters' Allocation: 4,500 (maximum in the Fosters Lager South Stand)

Club Colours: White with blue hoops shirts, white shorts
Nearest Railway Station: Reading (2.5 miles)
Parking (Car): 1,800-space car park at the ground, 700 of these spaces are reserved
Parking (Coach/Bus): As directed
Other Clubs Sharing Ground: London Irish RUFC
Police Force and Tel No: Thames Valley (0118 953 6000)
Disabled Visitors' Facilities:
  Wheelchairs: 128 designated spaces on all four sides of the ground
  Blind: 12 places for match day commentaries
Anticipated Development(s): The club has plans, if the need arises, to add an additional 5,000-seat section to the East Stand. Ultimately the ground could have a 40,000 capacity, but there is no timescale for this work.

KEY
C Club Offices
S Club Shop

↑ North direction (approx)

❶ North Stand
❷ East Stand
❸ South Stand (away)
❹ West Stand
❺ A33 Basingstoke Road
❻ A33 to M4 (Jct 11)
❼ A33 to Reading Town Centre and station (two miles)
❽ Hurst Way
❾ Boot End

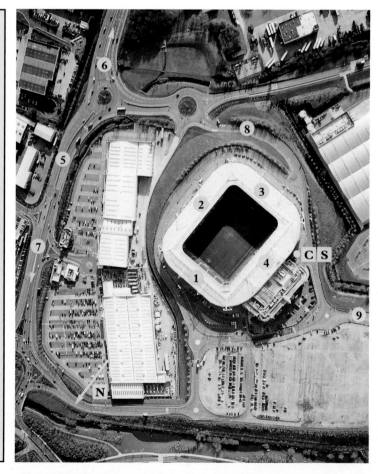

Above: 696931; *Right:* 696942

WEST (ULTIMA BUSINESS SOLUTIONS) STAND
UPPER
LOWER

PITCH SIZE
102 X 70 metres

SOUTH (FOSTERS LAGER) STAND
AWAY

NORTH (NPOWER) STAND

EAST (KYOCERA MITA) STAND

ACRE ROAD

With the club in the top six for most of the campaign, ultimately 2004/05 was to prove one of great disappointment for Steve Coppell and his Reading team. Vying with West Ham for the all-important sixth position as the season concluded on the last Sunday, Reading faced promotion-chasing Wigan Athletic at the JJB Stadium whilst West Ham faced the less daunting challenge of an away trip to Watford. The results — a 3-1 defeat for Reading combined with a 2-1 victory for West Ham — sent the London team into the Play-offs (and ultimately promotion to the Premier League) and consigned Reading to another campaign in the League Championship. In the final analysis, however, it was not the results at the end of the season that condemned Reading but a period after Christmas when the club failed to win in 11 games. Looking to 2005/06, provided that Coppell, a hugely experienced manager, is able to strengthen his squad over the season then, once again, Reading could be a force in the Championship.

ROCHDALE

Willbutts Lane, Spotland Stadium, Rochdale, OL11 5DS

Tel No: 01706 644648
Advance Tickets Tel No: 01706 644648
Fax: 01706 648466
Web-site: www.rochdaleafc.premiumtv.co.uk
E-Mail: office@rochdaleafc.co.uk
League: League Two
Brief History: Founded 1907 from former Rochadale Town F.C. (founded 1900). Founder-members Third Division North (1921). Record attendance 24,231
(Total) Current Capacity: 10,262 (8,342 seated) following completion of Pearl Street Stand
Visiting Supporters' Allocation: 3,650 (seated) in Willbutts Lane (Westrose Leisure) Stand

Club Colours: Blue shirts, blue shorts
Nearest Railway Station: Rochdale
Parking (Car): Rear of ground
Parking (Coach/Bus): Rear of ground
Other Clubs Sharing Ground: Rochdale Hornets RLFC
Police Force and Tel No: Greater Manchester (0161 872 5050)
Disabled Visitors' Facilities:
Wheelchairs: Main, WMG and Willbutts Lane stands – disabled area
Blind: Commentary available
Anticipated Development(s): None following completion of Willbutts Lane Stand.

KEY

C Club Offices
S Club Shop
E Entrance(s) for visiting supporters

⬆ North direction (approx)

❶ Willbutts Lane
❷ A627 Edenfield Road
❸ Rochdale BR Station (¹/₂ mile)
❹ Sandy Lane
❺ To M62
❻ To M65 and North
❼ Pearl Street (Westrose Leisure) Stand
❽ Willbutts Lane Stand

Above: 696966; Right: 696972

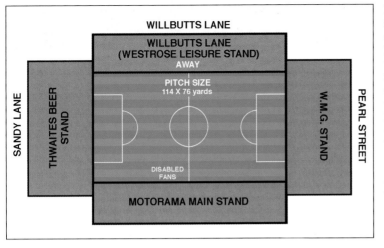

WILLBUTTS LANE

WILLBUTTS LANE
(WESTROSE LEISURE STAND)
AWAY

PITCH SIZE
114 X 76 yards

SANDY LANE

THWAITES BEER STAND

W.M.G. STAND

PEARL STREET

DISABLED FANS

MOTORAMA MAIN STAND

Having flirted with relegation to the Conference during the 2003/04 season, Rochdale seemed destined to face another battle to retain the club's League status in 2004/05. However, under the experienced Steve Parkin, the team prospered during the past season and ultimately finished a highly creditable ninth albeit well off the Play-offs in point terms (six adrift of Northampton in the all-important sixth place) with the squad's improved defence being one factor in this success. In terms of League Two, only four teams — all of whom finished in the top six — conceded fewer goals during the League campaign; Dale's problem was in scoring — only 54 being scored by the team. Provided that the team can maintain its defensive meanness and combine this with a better strike rate at the other end, there's every possibility that Rochdale could reach the Play-Offs at the end of 2005/06.

ROTHERHAM UNITED

Millmoor Ground, Millmoor Lane, Rotherham, S60 1HR

Tel No: 01709 512434
Advance Tickets Tel No: 0870 443 1884
Fax: 01709 512762
Web Site: www.themillers.premiumtv.co.uk
E-Mail: office@rotherhamunited.net
League: League One
Brief History: Founded 1877 (as Thornhill later Thornhill United), changed name to Rotherham County in 1905 and to Rotherham United in 1925 (amalgamated with Rotherham Town – Football League members 1893-97 – in 1925). Former Grounds include: Red House Ground and Clifton Lane Cricket Ground, moved to Millmoor in 1907. Record attendance 25,000
(Total) Current Capacity: 11,486 (6,949 seated)
Visiting Supporters' Allocation: 2,155 (all seated) in Railway End
Club Colours: Red shirts, white shorts
Nearest Railway Station: Rotherham Central

Parking (Car): Kimberworth and Main Street car parks, plus large car park adjacent to ground
Parking (Coach/Bus): As directed by Police
Police Force and Tel No: South Yorkshire (01709 371121)
Disabled Visitors' Facilities:
  Wheelchairs: Millmoor Lane
  Blind: Commentary available
Anticipated Developments(s): The club, having been taken over by a new consortium (Millers 05 Ltd), which was made up of club supporters and which wiped out £3 million of debt aided by the sale and lease back of Millmoor) in late December 2004, announced in February plans for the reconstruction of the Main Stand with a new 4,200-seat structure along with shops and offices in a £3.3million scheme. Formal planning permission for the scheme was granted at the end of April. It is hoped that the new stand will be completed for December 2005.

KEY
- **C** Club Offices
- **S** Club Shop
- **E** Entrance(s) for visiting supporters
- **R** Refreshment bars for visiting supporters
- **T** Toilets for visiting supporters

⬆ North direction (approx)

- ❶ Car Park
- ❷ To Rotherham Central BR Station
- ❸ A6109 Masborough Street
- ❹ Millmoor Lane
- ❺ To A6178 and M1 Junction 34
- ❻ A630 Centenary Way
- ❼ Station Road

Above: 698955; Right: 698958

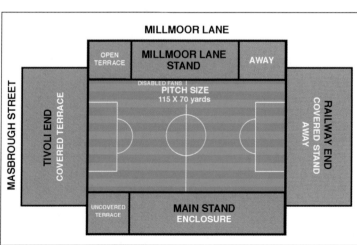

MILLMOOR LANE

MASBROUGH STREET			
	OPEN TERRACE	MILLMOOR LANE STAND	AWAY
TIVOLI END COVERED TERRACE	DISABLED FANS	PITCH SIZE 115 X 70 yards		RAILWAY END COVERED STAND AWAY
	UNCOVERED TERRACE	MAIN STAND ENCLOSURE	

After some seven years as manager at Millmoor, Ronnie Moore left the Millers at the end of January, with the team rooted to the bottom of the League Championship. One of the longest-serving managers in the Football League, Moore had overseen the Millers' rise from the League's basement division. However, appalling form saw the team win only three games in 2004/05 prior to his departure. Reserve coach Alan Knill, assisted by Mark Robins, was appointed but he couldn't stop the team's drift towards relegation. In early April, shortly after a 4-3 defeat at Ipswich confirmed the Millers' relegation, it was confirmed that Mick Harford was the new manager on a two-year contract. Now that the club's financial position is more secure, given the change of ownership, 2005/06 could be a season of consolidation and fans can perhaps expect a challenge for the Play-Offs at best.

RUSHDEN & DIAMONDS

Nene Park, Diamond Way, Irthlingborough, NN9 5QF

Tel No: 01933 652000
Advance Tickets Tel No: 01933 652936
Fax: 01933 650418
Web Site: www.thediamondsfc.premiumtv.co.uk
E-Mail: dean.howells@airwair.co.uk
League: League Two
Brief History: Rushden & Diamonds represents a merger between two teams — Rushden Town (founded in 1889) and Irthlingborough Diamonds (founded in 1946). The union, engineered by Max Griggs, occurred at the end of the 1991/92 season and from the start the club was based at the Nene Park ground of Irthlingborough Diamonds. Record attendance at Nene Park as a merged team 6,431
(Total) Current Capacity: 6,441 (4,641 seated)
Visiting Supporters' Allocation: 1,000 seats in the north side of the East (Air Wair) Stand (can be increased to 2,372 if needed)

Club Colours: White with red and blue trim shirts; blue shorts
Nearest Railway Station: Wellingborough (six miles)
Parking (Car): 1,000 spaces at ground
Parking (Coach/Bus): As directed by the police
Police Force and Tel No: Northamptonshire (01933 440333)
Disabled Visitors' Facilities:
  Wheelchairs: 22 Places in the North Stand allocated to season ticket holders; 12 in the South Stand — limited number available on match by match basis
  Blind: No special facility
Anticipated Development(s): None

KEY

⬆ North direction (approx)

❶ A6 Station Road
❷ To Rushden
❸ To Kettering
❹ Station Road (old)
❺ B5348 Station Road to Irthlingborough
❻ Diamond Way
❼ River Nene

Above: 697272; *Right:* 697263

Appointed towards the end of the 2004/05 season Ernie Tippett was unable to prevent the team's drop into League Two. Unfortunately, the club's continued poor form, despite the occasional success (such as a 1-0 victory away at League One Bradford City in the first round of the FA Cup), saw the team dragged towards the relegation zone. In mid-January, with the team five points off the bottom and with only six league victories in 35 games since his appointment, Tippett was sacked. Barry Hunter was appointed as caretaker and under his control, League Two safety was secured with a number of impressive results (including a 2-0 victory over future champions Yeovil Town). At the end of the season, control of the club was passed to a supporters' trust as ex-chairman Max Griggs ceded control.

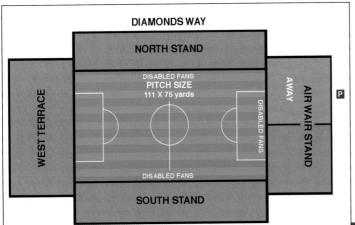

Under Griggs, the club had developed significantly, but increasing financial problems with his other businesses had adversely affected the team and had been one factor in its relegation at the end of 2003/04. Whilst the trust establishes itself and the club adjusts to life without Max Griggs, it's hard to escape the conclusion that the new season will be one of consolidation at Nene Park.

SCUNTHORPE UNITED

Glanford Park, Doncaster Road, Scunthorpe DN15 8TD

Tel No: 01724 848077
Advance Tickets Tel No: 01724 848077
Fax: 01724 857986
Web Site: www.scunthorpe-united.premiumtv.co.uk
E-mail: admin@scunthorpe-united.co.uk
League: League One
Brief History: Founded 1899 as Scunthorpe United, amalgamated with North Lindsey to become 'Scunthorpe & Lindsey United' in 1912. Changed name to Scunthorpe United in 1956. Former Grounds: Crosby (Lindsey United) and Old Showground, moved to Glanford Park in 1988. Elected to Football League in 1950. Record attendance 8,775 (23,935 at Old Showground)
(Total) Current Capacity: 9,200 (6,400 seated)
Visiting Supporters' Allocation: 1,678 (all seated) in South (Caparo Merchant Bar) Stand

Club Colours: Claret and blue shirts, claret shorts
Nearest Railway Station: Scunthorpe
Parking (Car): At ground
Parking (Coach/Bus): At ground
Police Force and Tel No: Humberside (01724 282888)
Disabled Visitors' Facilities:
  Wheelchairs: County Chef Stand
  Blind: Commentary available
Anticipated Development(s): Although a new stadium – Glanford Park opened in 1988 – there is a possibility that, in the future, the existing Evening Telegraph Stand will be demolished and replaced by a two-tier structure.

KEY

C Club Offices
S Club Shop
E Entrance(s) for visiting supporters
R Refreshment bars for visiting supporters
T Toilets for visiting supporters

↑ North direction (approx)

❶ Car Park
❷ Evening Telegraph Stand
❸ A18 to Scunthorpe BR Station and Town Centre (1½ miles)
❹ M181 and M180 Junction 3

Above: 697516; *Right:* 697507

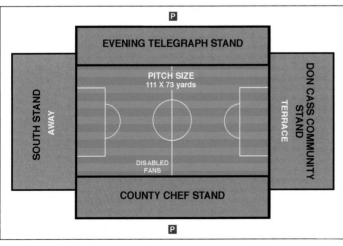

P

EVENING TELEGRAPH STAND

PITCH SIZE
111 X 73 yards

SOUTH STAND
AWAY

DON CASS COMMUNITY
STAND

TERRACE

DISABLED
FANS

COUNTY CHEF STAND

P

What a difference a season makes. At the end of 2003/04 Scunthorpe were battling to stay in League Two, after a disastrous season, but at the end of 2004/05 Brian Laws' Iron had secured second place and automatic promotion to League One. It was a close run thing, however, as the club could have finished in fourth place — and thus faced the Play-Offs — if results had gone against them on the final Saturday. In the event, a 0-0 draw with Shrewsbury Town at the Gay Meadow combined with Southend's 1-1 draw at Grimsby ensured that United were promoted. This is not the first time that Scunthorpe has achieved promotion under Laws and his struggle this time, as before, will be to ensure that the club consolidates its position in League One. Probably one of the pre-season favourites for relegation, Iron will have a battle to retain its new-found status in 2005/06.

SHEFFIELD UNITED

Bramall Lane, Sheffield, S2 4SU

Tel No: 0870 787 1960
Advance Tickets Tel No: 0870 787 1799
Fax: 0870 787 3345
Web Site: www.sufc.premiumtv.co.uk
E-Mail: info@sufc.co.uk
League: League Championship
Brief History: Founded 1889. (Sheffield Wednesday occasionally used Bramall Lane c1880.) Founder-members 2nd Division (1892). Record attendance 68,287
(Total) Current Capacity: 30,936 (all seated)
Visiting Supporters' Allocation: 2,700 (seated) can be increased to 5,200 if needed
Club Colours: Red and white striped shirts, black shorts

Nearest Railway Station: Sheffield Midland
Parking (Car): Street parking
Parking (Coach/Bus): As directed by Police
Police Force and Tel No: South Yorkshire (0114 276 8522)
Disabled Visitors' Facilities:
   Wheelchairs: South Stand
   Blind: Commentary available
Anticipated Development(s): The club is contemplating construction of a corner stand, located between the Laver and Bramall stands, although there is no confirmed timescale for the work. This will add 1,500 seats to the ground capacity.

KEY

C Club Offices
S Club Shop
E Entrance(s) for visiting supporters

↑ North direction (approx)

❶ A621 Bramall Lane
❷ Shoreham Street
❸ Car Park
❹ Sheffield Midland BR Station (¹/₄ mile)
❺ John Street
❻ Spion Stand
❼ John Street Stand
❽ St Mary's Road

Above: 697175; *Right:* 697169

Ultimately a disappointing season for Neil Warnock and the Blades saw the team finish in eighth position for the second year running in the Championship some six points adrift of the all-important sixth place. Despite a strengthened squad, United's failure to progress in the league is all the more galling considering the club's prowess against Premier League opponents in the cup competitions. Yet again, in 2004/05, the Blades demonstrated their fearsome cup skills in defeating Aston Villa at Brammall Lane and drawing with Arsenal at Highbury (before losing the reply at home against the London side on penalties).

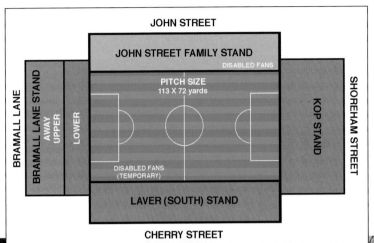

The close season will undoubtedly see Warnock endeavour to strengthen the squad but it's hard to escape the conclusion that perhaps the Play-Offs are the best that the team can hope to make with, perhaps, again a good run in one of the cup competitions. There is also the small issue of ensuring local supremacy now that Wednesday are now back in the same division.

SHEFFIELD WEDNESDAY

Hillsborough, Sheffield, S6 1SW

Tel No: 0114 221 2121
Advance Tickets Tel No: 0114 221 2400
Fax: 0114 221 2122
Web Site: www.swfc.premiumtv.co.uk
E-Mail: enquiries@swfc.co.uk
League: League Championship
Brief History: Founded 1867 as The
Wednesday F.C. (changed to Sheffield
Wednesday c1930). Former Grounds: London
Road, Wyrtle Road (Heeley), Sheaf House
Ground, Encliffe & Olive Grove (Bramall Lane
also used occasionally), moved to Hillsborough
(then named 'Owlerton' in 1899). Founder-
members Second Division (1892). Record
attendance 72,841

(Total) Current Capacity: 39,859 (all seated)
Visiting Supporters' Allocation: 3,700 (all
seated) in West Stand Upper
Club Colours: Blue and white striped shirts,
black shorts
Nearest Railway Station: Sheffield (4 miles)
Parking (Car): Street Parking
Parking (Coach/Bus): Owlerton Stadium
Police Force and Tel No: South Yorkshire
(0114 276 8522)
Disabled Visitors' Facilities:
Wheelchairs: North and Lower West Stands
Blind: Commentary available

KEY

C Club Offices
E Entrance(s) for visiting
supporters

↑ North direction (approx)

❶ Leppings Lane
❷ River Don
❸ A61 Penistone Road North
❹ Sheffield BR Station and
City Centre (4 miles)
❺ Spion Kop
❻ To M1 (North)
❼ To M1 (South)
❽ West Stand

Above: 697186; Right: 697177

Despite considerable strengthening of the squad during the close season, the Owls' poor start to the campaign — 12 points from the first nine games — saw Chris Turner, manager for almost two years, dismissed in mid-September. The club announced later the following week the appointment of ex-Southampton boss Paul Sturrock as the new manager; Sturrock had success at this level with Plymouth before his ill-fated short stint at Saints. The appointment proved to be astute as, under Sturrock's management, the Owls secured fifth place, despite a last day defeat at Hillsborough by Bristol City, and thus a place in the Play-Offs. Victory 1-0 at home in the semi-finals against Brentford allied to a 2-1 victory at Griffin Park took Wednesday to the Millennium Stadium and a final against Hartlepool. Whilst Wednesday dominated much of the game, Hartlepool were leading 2-1 as the game entered its final 10 minutes; however, with Hartlepool's Chris Westwood being sent off and with Wednesday converting the resulting penalty, the game went to extra time with the Owls ultimately being victorious 4-2. Thus League Championship football beckons for 2005/06 along with local derbies against United and Leeds. Ironically, for Sturrock, Southampton will also feature as opponents and the Sheffield manager may be permitted a wry smile for this. Sturrock has proved a capable manager at this level and Wednesday should have the potential to consolidate their League Championship status although, as a promoted team through the Play-offs, the club will need to dig deep to avoid being sucked into the relegation battle.

SHREWSBURY TOWN

Gay Meadow, Shrewsbury, SY2 6AB

Tel No: 01743 360111
Advance Tickets Tel No: 01743 360111
Fax: 01743 236384
Web-site: www.shrewsburytown.co.uk
E-mail: clubshop@shrewsburytown.co.uk
League: League Two
Brief History: Founded 1886. Former Grounds: Monkmoor Racecourse, Ambler's Field and The Barracks Ground (moved to Gay Meadow 1910). Elected to Football League 1950; relegated to Nationwide Conference at end of 2002/03 and promoted back to the Football League, via the Play-Offs, at the end of 2003/04. Record attendance 18,917
(Total) Current Capacity: 8,000 (2,500 seated)
Visiting Supporters' Allocation: 2,500 (500 seated) in the Station End (standing) and Main Stand (seated)
Club Colours: Blue shirts and blue shorts

Nearest Railway Station: Shrewsbury
Parking (Car): Adjacent car park
Parking(Coach/Bus): Gay Meadow
Police Force and Tel No: West Mercia (01743 232888)
Disabled Visitors' Facilities:
    Wheelchairs: Alongside pitch (as directed)
    Blind: No special facility
Anticipated Development(s): Planning Permission for the redevelopment of the Gay Meadow as housing once the club relocates was given by the council in October 2004. Permission has also been granted for the construction of the new 10,000-seat ground, scheduled to be complete during the 2005/06 season, at Oteley Road and preliminary work has already commenced. Thus the 2005/06 season will see the last games for the Shrews' at the club's home since 1910.

KEY

C Club Offices

S Club Shop

E Entrance(s) for visiting supporters

R Refreshment bars for visiting supporters

T Toilets for visiting supporters

⬆ North direction (approx)

❶ Entrance road to ground
❷ Abbey Foregate
❸ River Severn
❹ Car Parks
❺ Shrewsbury BR Station (1 mile – shortest route)
❻ Riverside Terrace
❼ English Bridge
❽ Wyle Cop
❾ Station End (away)
❿ Wakeman End
⓫ Wakeman/Centre/Station Stand
⓬ Old Potts Way (all routes via ring road)

Above: 697458; Right: 697454

With the Shrews propping up League Two towards the end of October, after a disappointing start to the season, Jimmy Quinn resigned as manager. Following the triumph of regaining the club's league status following victory in the Play-Off final at the Britannia Stadium, Town had struggled to make an impact at the higher level and Quinn felt that the club needed a change after his 18 months in charge. Chic Bates took over as caretaker, guiding the Shrews to a 1-1 draw in his first game. However, in mid-November, with the Shrews having just suffered an embarrassing 2-0 defeat in the FA Cup First Round away at non-league Histon, it was announced that ex-Preston and Exeter boss Gary Peters would be taking over the Gay Meadow hot-seat. Under Peters the team's position stabilised and League Two survival was assured. However, the ultimate points total of 49 suggests that the Shrews will again struggle in League Two in 2005/06 unless Peters can significantly improve his squad.

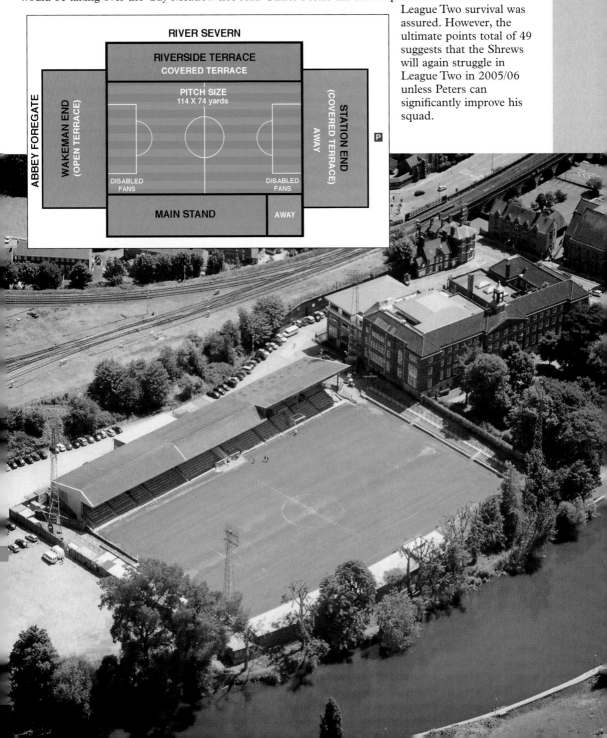

RIVER SEVERN

RIVERSIDE TERRACE
COVERED TERRACE

PITCH SIZE
114 X 74 yards

ABBEY FOREGATE

WAKEMAN END
(OPEN TERRACE)

STATION END
(COVERED TERRACE)
AWAY

DISABLED FANS

DISABLED FANS

MAIN STAND

AWAY

P

SOUTHAMPTON

The Friends Provident St Mary's Stadium, Britannia Road, Southampton SO14 5FP

Tel No: 0870 22 00 000
Advance Tickets Tel No: 0870 2200150
Fax: 02380 727727
Web Site: www.saintsfc.co.uk
E-Mail: tellrupert@saintsfc.co.uk
League: League Championship
Brief History: Founded 1885 as 'Southampton St. Mary's Young Men's Association (changed name to Southampton in 1897). Former Grounds: Northlands Road, Antelope Ground, County Ground, moved to The Dell in 1898 and to St Mary's Stadium in 2001. Founder members Third Division (1920). Record attendance (at The Dell) 31,044 (at St Mary's) 32,151
(Total) Current Capacity: 32,251 (all-seated)

Visiting Supporters' Allocation: c3,200 in North Stand
Club Colours: Red and white shirts, black shorts
Nearest Railway Station: Southampton Central
Parking (Car): Street parking or town centre car parks
Parking (Coach/Bus): As directed by the police
Police Force and Tel No: Hampshire (02380 335444)
Disabled Visitors' Facilities:
   Wheelchairs: c200 places
   Blind: Commentary available
Anticipated Development(s): Following completion of the new stadium the club has no further plans at present.

KEY

C Club Offices
S Club Shop
E Entrance(s) for visiting supporters

↑ North direction (approx)

❶ A3024 Northam Road
❷ B3028 Britannia Road
❸ River Itchen
❹ To M27 (five miles)
❺ To Southampton Central station and town centre
❻ Marine Parade
❼ To A3025 (and Itchen toll bridge)
❽ Belvedere Road
❾ North Stand

Above: 699202; Right: 699209

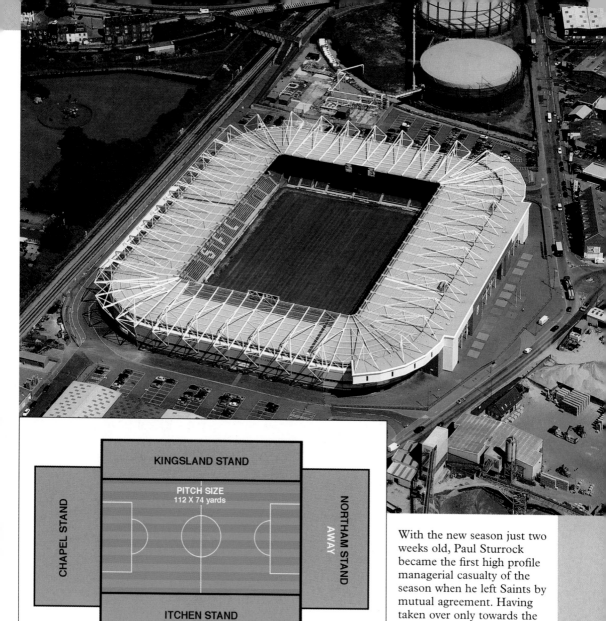

KINGSLAND STAND

PITCH SIZE
112 X 74 yards

CHAPEL STAND

NORTHAM STAND
AWAY

ITCHEN STAND

BRITANNIA ROAD

With the new season just two weeks old, Paul Sturrock became the first high profile managerial casualty of the season when he left Saints by mutual agreement. Having taken over only towards the end of 2003/04, Sturrock had managed the team for only 13 games but, despite a 3-2 victory in his final game in charge, the 'negative and unfair media coverage' led to his departure. He was replaced as caretaker by Steve Wigley. However, Saints' form under Wigley was little short of disastrous and, following a period of uncertainty, ex-Pompey boss Harry Redknapp, assisted by Jim Smith, moved in during early December with Wigley departing from the club. Under Redknapp the club's form improved with striker Peter Crouch coming to the fore and, come the last Sunday of the season, any one of the four teams in the relegation battle could have survived. Unfortunately for Saints' fans, with Crouch suspended and with Manchester United the opponents, the odds were stacked against Saints. Losing 2-1 in the final game resulted in the team finishing last and being relegated, thus ending Southampton's presence in the top flight after some 27 years. After the end of the season, it was confirmed that Redknapp would remain manager in 2005/06. Whilst Saints will undoubtedly feature in the promotion battle, how close the team comes to making an automatic return will depend on how many key players depart during the close season and the squad that Redknapp is able to build for the Championship.

SOUTHEND UNITED

Roots Hall Ground, Victoria Avenue, Southend-on-Sea, SS2 6NQ

Tel No: 0870 174 2000
Advance Tickets Tel No: 0870 174 2001
Fax: 01702 304124
Web Site: www.southendunited.premiumtv.co.uk
E-mail: info@southend-united.co.uk
League: League One
Brief History: Founded 1906. Former
  Grounds: Roots Hall, Kursaal, the Stadium
  Grainger Road, moved to Roots Hall (new
  Ground) 1955. Founder-members Third
  Division (1920). Record attendance 31,033
(Total) Current Capacity: 12,392 (all seated)
Visiting Supporters' Allocation: 2,700
  (maximum) (all seated) in North Stand and
  North West Enclosure
Club Colours: Blue shirts, blue shorts
Nearest Railway Station: Prittlewell

Parking (Car): Street parking
Parking (Coach/Bus): Car park at Ground
Police Force and Tel No: Essex (01702 431212)
Disabled Visitors' Facilities:
  Wheelchairs: West Stand
  Blind: Commentary available
Anticipated Development(s): In early May
  2004 it was announced that the local council
  had backed plans for the construction of the
  proposed new 16,000-seat stadium costing
  £12.5 million. The club is now awaiting final
  planning permission for the construction of the
  new ground at Fossetts Farm. At this stage,
  there is no timescale, but it would certainly
  appear that after some years of uncertainty that
  Roots Hall is now living on borrowed time.

KEY

C Club Offices
E Entrance(s) for visiting
  supporters
R Refreshment bars for visiting
  supporters
T Toilets for visiting supporters

⬆ North direction (approx)

❶ Director's Car Park
❷ Prittlewell BR Station
  (¼ mile)
❸ A127 Victoria Aveneue
❹ Fairfax Drive
❺ Southend centre (½ mile)
❻ North (Universal Cycles)
  Stand

156

SHAKESPEARE DRIVE

C2C WEST STAND

AWAY

ROOTS HALL AVENUE

HI-TEC (SOUTH) STAND

UPPER TIER

LOWER TIER

DISABLED FANS

PITCH SIZE
110 X 74 yards

VISUALLY IMPAIRED

NORTH STAND

AWAY

FAIRFAX DRIVE

BLACK | GREEN | RED | YELLOW | BLUE

GKC EAST STAND

VICTORIA AVENUE

Few teams visit the Millennium Stadium once in a season, but Steve Tilson's United made two visits during what proved, ultimately, to be a successful campaign in 2004/05. However, it might have been very different had the club not come out victorious in the Play-Off final, defeating Lincoln City 2-0 after extra time. The club's first visit, for the final of the LDV Vans Trophy, proved a disappointment as the club lost in the final again, this time to Wrexham. In the league, the team was also to suffer last day disappointment when, as one of three teams chasing the last two automatic promotion places, the Shrimpers, having drawn 1-1 at Grimsby, were pipped by Swansea — 1-0 victors at Bury — and Scunthorpe — who drew 0-0 at Shrewsbury. In the Play-Off semi-finals, the club was drawn against Northampton Town, one of the pre-season favourites for promotion, but victory over the two legs ensured another visit to Cardiff. The club's two previous trips to the Millennium Stadium had both resulted in defeat and so it was third time lucky. Now facing the challenge of League One football, consolidation will be the name of the game in 2005/06.

STOCKPORT COUNTY

Edgeley Park, Hardcastle Road, Edgeley, Stockport, SK3 9DD

Tel No: 0161 286 8888
Advance Tickets Tel No: 0161 286 8888
Fax: 0161 286 8900
Web Site: www.stockportcounty.premiumtv.co.uk
E-Mail: martin.booker@stockportcounty.com
League: League Two
Brief History: Founded 1883 as Heaton Norris
Rovers, changed name to Stockport County in 1890.
Former Grounds: Heaton Norris Recreation
Ground, Heaton Norris Wanderers Cricket Ground,
Chorlton's Farm, Ash Inn Ground, Wilkes Field
(Belmont Street) and Nursery Inn (Green Lane),
moved to Edgeley Park in 1902. Record attendance
27,833
(Total) Current Capacity: 11,541 (all seated)
Visiting Supporters' Allocation: 800 (all seated) in
Vernon Stand (can be increased by 1,300 all-seated
on open Railway End if needed)
Club Colours: Blue with white stripe shirts, blue
shorts

Nearest Railway Station: Stockport
Parking (Car): Street Parking
Parking (Coach/Bus): As directed by Police
Other Clubs Sharing Ground: Sale Sharks RUFC
Police Force and Tel No: Greater Manchester (0161
872 5050)
Disabled Visitors' Facilities:
  Wheelchairs: Main and Cheadle stands
  Blind: Headsets available
Anticipated Development(s): Although the club is
still planning for the reconstruction of the Railway
End, with the intention of constructing a new 5,500-
seat capacity stand on the site, there is no time scale
for this work (which had originally been planned for
1999/2000). Theoretically, the next phase after the
Railway End would be an upgrade to the Vernon BS
Stand, with the intention of making the ground's
capacity 20,000.

KEY

C Club Offices
E Entrance(s) for visiting
supporters

⬆ North direction (approx)

❶ Mercian Way
❷ Hardcastle Road
❸ Stockport BR station (1/4
mile)
❹ Railway End
❺ Main Stand
❻ Cheadle Stand
❼ Vernon BS Stand

Above: 695712; *Right:* 695706

VERNON BS STAND

AWAY

RAILWAY END
UNCOVERED TERRACE

PITCH SIZE
111 X 71 yards

CHEADLE STAND

DISABLED
FANS

MAIN STAND

P HARDCASTLE ROAD

Despite Sammy McIlroy's experience of management at this level he was unable to prevent County's drift into the League One relegation zone and, towards the end of November, he departed from the managerial hot seat. Initially, the club made Mark Lillis caretaker manager, but in mid-December ex-Sheffield Wednesday boss Chris Turner took over with the team still rooted to the bottom of League One. In reality changing the boss mid-season proved to be merely delaying the inevitable, although there were some encouraging performances. County remained rooted to the bottom of League One with the result that League Two football will be on offer in 2005/06. As with all relegated teams, the club should be able to prosper at this lower level and make a serious challenge for the Play-Offs at least.

STOKE CITY

Britannia Stadium, Stanley Matthews Way, Stoke-on-Trent ST4 4EG

Tel No: 01782 592222
Advance Tickets Tel No: 01782 592204
Fax: 01782 592220
Web Site: www.stokecityfc.premiumtv.co.uk
E-Mail: info@stokecityfc.com
League: League Championship
Brief History: Founded 1863 as Stoke F.C., amalgamated with Stoke Victoria in 1878, changed to Stoke City in 1925. Former Grounds: Sweetings Field, Victoria Ground (1878-1997), moved to new ground for start of 1997/98 season. Record attendance (at Victoria Ground): 51,380; at Britannia Stadium 28,218
(Total) Current Capacity: 28,383 (all-seater)
Visiting Supporters' Allocation: 4,800 (in the South Stand)
Club Colours: Red and white striped shirts, white shorts
Nearest Railway Station: Stoke-on-Trent

Parking (Car): The 650 parking spaces at the ground are for officials and guests only. The 1,600 spaces in the South car park are pre-booked only, with the majority held by season ticket holders. There is some on-street parking, but with a 10-15min walk.
Parking (Coach/Bus): As directed
Police Force and Tel No: Staffordshire (01782 744644)
Disabled Visitors' Facilities:
  Wheelchairs: 164 places for disabled spectators
  Blind: Commentaries available
Anticipated Development(s): There are long-term plans to increase the ground's to 30,000 by the construction of a corner stand between the John Smith Stand and the Boothen End but there is no timescale for this work.

KEY

↑ North direction (approx)

❶ A50
❷ To Stoke BR station
❸ To A500 Queensway and City Centre, railway station and M6
❹ North Stand
❺ West Stand
❻ East Stand
❼ South Stand (away)
❽ To Uttoxeter

Above: 698966; *Right:* 698973

Another season of mid-table mediocrity for Stoke City saw the team finish the League Championship season in 12th position, as opposed to 11th in 2003/04, almost exactly equidistant in points terms between the Play-Offs and the drop zone. But for some of the season it appeared that the team could do much better as it hovered just below the Play-Off zone. At the end of the season, the club decided to dispense with the services of experienced boss Tony Pulis — apparently for his inability to exploit the international market place for players — with the Dutchman Johan Boskamp being appointed as replacement. In terms of international knowledge, Boskamp is certainly better connected and it will be

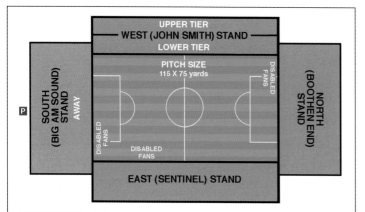

interesting to see if these connections lead to new talent heading to the Britannia Stadium. If he succeeds then Stoke could emerge as a surprise package in the Championship during 2005/06, if not, then probably another season of mid-table anonymity beckons.

SUNDERLAND

Stadium of Light, Sunderland, SR5 1SU

Tel No: 0191 551 5000
Advance Tickets Tel No: 0191 551 5151
Fax: 0191 551 5123
Web Site: www.safc.com
E-Mail: Via Website
League: F.A. Premier
Brief History: Founded 1879 as 'Sunderland & District Teachers Association', changed to 'Sunderland Association' in 1880 and shortly after to 'Sunderland'. Former Grounds: Blue House Field, Groves Field (Ashbrooke), Horatio Street, Abbs Field, Newcastle Road and Roker Park (1898-1997); moved to Stadium of Light for the start of the 1997/98 season. Record crowd (at Roker Park): 75,118; at Stadium of Light (48,353)
(Total) Current Capacity: 48,353 all-seater
Visiting Supporters' Allocation: 3,000 (South Stand)
Club Colours: Red and white striped shirts, black shorts
Nearest Railway Station: Stadium of Light (Tyne & Wear Metro

Parking (Car): Car park at ground reserved for season ticket holders. Limited on-street parking (but the police may decide to introduce restrictions). Otherwise off-street parking in city centre
Parking (Coach/Bus): As directed
Police Force and Tel No: Tyne & Wear (0191 510 2020)
Disabled Visitors' Facilities:
  Wheelchairs: 180 spots
  Blind: Commentary available
Anticipated Development(s): When the club was last in the Premier league it had plans to increase capacity at the Stadium of Light by adding 7,200 seats in an expanded Metro FM Stand and a further 9,000 in a second tier to the McEwans Stand, taking the ground's capacity ultimately to 64,000. These were put 'on ice' following relegation. Now the club has regained its Premier League status it will be interesting to see if these plans are resurrected.

KEY

C Club Offices
S Club Shop
E Entrance(s) for visiting supporters

↑ North direction (approx)

❶ River Wear
❷ North (McEwans) Stand
❸ South (Metro FM) Stand (away)
❹ To Sunderland BR station (0.5 mile)
❺ Southwick Road
❻ Stadium Way
❼ Millennium Way
❽ Hay Street
❾ To Wearmouth Bridge (via A1018 North Bridge Street) to City Centre

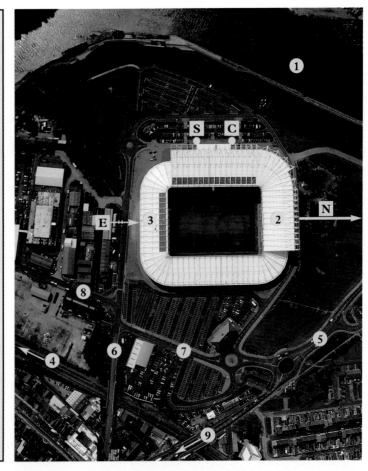

Above: 699151; *Right:* 699159

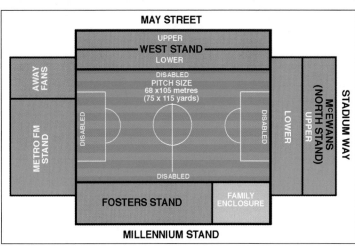

MAY STREET

UPPER
WEST STAND
LOWER

AWAY FANS

METRO FM STAND

DISABLED

DISABLED
PITCH SIZE
68 x105 metres
(75 x 115 yards)

DISABLED

DISABLED

FOSTERS STAND

FAMILY ENCLOSURE

MILLENNIUM STAND

LOWER

McEWANS
(NORTH STAND)
UPPER

STADIUM WAY

One of three teams to dominate the League Championship in 2004/05, Mick McCarthy's Sunderland ultimately proved by far the strongest team in the competition securing the Championship well before the end of the season and, ultimately, finishing seven points clear of second place Wigan. Thus Premier League football is restored to Wearside after a gap of two seasons. The Black Cats have the tradition and fan base to succeed in the Premiership, as they have done in the past, and in McCarthy an experienced manager who should be capable of keeping them up. However, the gap in quality between the Championship and the Premier League seems to get greater each year and it's inevitable that any team promoted will struggle to stay up. Finishing above the drop zone will probably be regarded as success by Sunderland.

SWANSEA CITY

New Stadium, Landore, Swansea SA1 2FA

Telephone: 01792 616600
Advance Tickets Tel No: 0870 040004
Fax: 01792 616606
Web site: www.swanseacity.premiumtv.co.uk
E-mail: dawn@swanseacityfc.co.uk
League: League One
Brief History: Founded 1900 as Swansea Town, changed to Swansea City in 1970. Former grounds: various, including Recreation Ground, and Vetch Field (1912-2005); moved to the new ground for the start of the 2005/06 season. Founder-members Third Division (1920). Record attendance (at Vetch Field): 32,796.
(Total) Current Capacity: 20,500
Visiting Supporters' Allocation: 3,500 maximum in North Stand
Club Colours: white shirts, white shorts
Nearest Railway Station: Swansea

Parking (Car): Adjacent to ground
Parking (Coach/Bus): As directed
Other Clubs Sharing Ground: Swansea Ospreys RUFC
Police Force and Tel No: South Wales (01792 456999)
Disabled Visitors' Facilities:
  Wheelchairs: tbc
  Blind: tbc
Anticipated Development(s): After several years of uncertainty, Swansea City relocated to the new White Rock Stadium with its 20,000 all-seater capacity for the start of the 2005/06 season. The ground, which cost £25 million to construct and which was built on the site of the old Morfa stadium, will be shared by the Swansea Ospreys RUFC team.

KEY

⬆ North direction (approx)

❶ A4067 Ffordd Cwm Tawe Road
❷ A4067 to A48 and M4 Junction 44 (five miles)
❸ B4603 Neath Road
❹ Brunel Way
❺ Normandy Road
❻ A4217
❼ To Swansea city centre and BR railway station (two miles)
❽ Parking
❾ Cardiff-Swansea railway line

Above: 698594; Right: 698599

City's last season at the Vetch Field proved to be one of considerable success on the field as Kenny Jackett's team was one of the leading candidates for promotion all campaign, although it was only with results on the last day that promotion, as third in League Two, was confirmed. As the last Saturday dawned, City were in third place, on goal difference from Southend, but if Southend's result was better than Swansea's then the Essex team would have grabbed the final automatic promotion spot. In the event, City triumphed 1-0 at Bury whilst Southend were held to a 1-1 draw. Thus the new stadium will see League One football. As with all promoted teams there will be a struggle to consolidate at the higher level, but with the new ground in place confidence and expectations will be high and City certainly has the potential to achieve a top-half position at the very least.

FFORDD CWM TAWE ROAD

WEST STAND

BRUNEL WAY

SOUTH STAND (FAMILY)

NORTH STAND (AWAY)

EAST STAND

SWINDON TOWN

County Ground, County Road, Swindon, SN1 2ED

Tel No: 0870 443 1969
Advance Tickets Tel No: 0870 443 1894
Fax: 01793 333703
Web Site: www.swindontownfc.premiumtv.co.uk
E-Mail: enquiries@swindontownfc.co.uk
League: League One
Brief History: Founded 1881. Former Grounds: Quarry Ground, Globe Road, Croft Ground, County Ground (adjacent to current Ground and now Cricket Ground), moved to current County Ground in 1896. Founder-members Third Division (1920). Record attendance 32,000
(Total) Current Capacity: 15,700 (all seated)
Visiting Supporters' Allocation: 3,342 (all seated) in Arkell's Stand and Stratton Bank (open)
Club Colours: Red shirts, white shorts

Nearest Railway Station: Swindon
Parking (Car): Town Centre
Parking (Coach/Bus): Adjacent car park
Police Force and Tel No: Wiltshire (01793 528111)
Disabled Visitors' Facilities:
  Wheelchairs: In front of Arkell's Stand
  Blind: Commentary available
Anticipated Development(s): The proposed relocation to the west of the town, at Shaw Tip, was thwarted in July 2004 when the local council decided not to sacrifice the community forest located at the site. The failure of the proposed move, which had been opposed by residents and many fans, resulted in the club seeking planning permission to redevelop its existing ground in February 2005.

KEY
C Club Offices
S Club Shop
E Entrance(s) for visiting supporters

North direction (approx)
1   Shrivenham Road
2 Stratton Bank (away)
3 A345 Queens Drive (M4 Junction 15 – 3½ miles)
4 Swindon BR Station (½ mile)
5 Town End
6 Car Park
7 County Cricket Ground
8 Nationwide Stand
9 Arkell's Stand
10 'Magic' Roundabout

Above: 699231; Right: 699234

COUNTY ROAD

TOWN END (OVERFLOW)

ARKELLS STAND

AR1	FAM	AR3	AR4	
KIDS	AR2	ENCLOSURE		AWAY

DISABLED FANS

PITCH SIZE
114 X 74 yards

DISABLED FANS

ENCLOSURE

NW6	NW5	NW4	NW3	NW2	NW1

SOUTH STAND

SHRIVENHAM ROAD

STRATTON BANK STAND (OPEN STAND) **AWAY**

Having finished in fifth place at the end of 2003/04 and having just lost out in the Play-Offs, hopes were high at the County Ground that 2004/05 would again see the team threaten for the Play-offs at worst. In the event, however, Andy King's team was unable to maintain the progress made in the previous season and had to be content with a position of mid-table mediocrity, ultimately finishing in 12th position. That the club achieved this position is all the more remarkable considering that King was constrained throughout the season by financial problems and this will undoubtedly be a continuing factor in 2005/06 as a number of players will leave during the summer and King will find it hard to replace them. Much will depend for the new season on how the club replaces top-scorer Sam Parkin; his 24 goals were crucial to Swindon's season and, without him, the club could struggle to retain its League One status.

TORQUAY UNITED

Plainmoor Ground, Torquay, TQ1 3PS

Tel No: 01803 328666
Advance Tickets Tel No: 01803 328666
Fax: 01803 323976
Web Site: www.torquayunited.premiumtv.co.uk
E-Mail: gulls@aol.com
League: League Two
Brief History: Founded 1898, as Torquay United, amalgamated with Ellacombe in 1910, changed name to Torquay Town. Amalgamated with Babbacombe in 1921, changed name to Torquay United. Former Grounds: Teignmouth Road, Torquay Recreation Ground, Cricketfield Road & Torquay Cricket Ground, moved to Plainmoor (Ellacombe Ground) in 1910. Record attendance 21,908
(Total) Current Capacity: 6,283 (2,446 seated)
Visiting Supporters' Allocation: 1,004 (plus 196 seated in Main Stand)

Club Colours: Yellow with white stripe shirts, yellow shorts
Nearest Railway Station: Torquay (2 miles)
Parking (Car): Street parking
Parking (Coach/Bus): Lymington Road coach station
Police Force and Tel No: Devon & Cornwall (01803 214491)
Disabled Visitors' Facilities:
  Wheelchairs: Ellacombe End
  Blind: Commentary available
Anticipated Development(s): There are proposals for a joint project with a local school for the rebuilding of the Main Stand. This would give United a 2,500-seat stand but there is no confirmed timescale.

KEY

C Club Offices
S Club Shop
E Entrance(s) for visiting supporters
R Refreshment bars for visiting supporters
T Toilets for visiting supporters

↑ North direction (approx)

❶ Warbro Road
❷ B3202 Marychurch Road
❸ Marnham Road
❹ Torquay BR Station (2 miles)
❺ To A38
❻ Sparkworld End

Above: 692266; *Right:* 692257

Having seized automatic promotion on the last day of the 2003/04 season, life was potentially a struggle for the Gulls in League One and so it proved although it was to the credit of Leroy Rosenior's squad that it was drawn out again until the last day of the season. What is it with Torquay that means that everything comes down to the last match of the season — remember the crunch match some years ago where victory over Barnet at Underhill sent the home team into the Conference and ensured Torquay's League survival. On this occasion, Torquay had destiny in their own hands: a point from the away game at Colchester would ensure survival whatever happened to Milton Keynes Dons and Oldham. In the event, the Gulls were defeated 2-1 and this, combined with victories for both Oldham and Milton Keynes, meant that League Two football will be on the menu at Plainmoor in 2005/06. Potentially, however, provided that he can keep much of the squad together, Rosenior has proved that he can take the team up a division and so it's probable that Torquay will be one of the favourites for the Play-Offs at least.

TOTTENHAM HOTSPUR

Bill Nicholson Way, 748 High Road, Tottenham, London N17 0AP

Tel No: 0208 365 5000
Ticket Line: 0870 420 5000
Fax: 020 8365 5005
Web Site: www.spurs.co.uk
E-Mail: email@spurs.co.uk
League: F.A. Premier
Brief History: Founded 1882 as 'Hotspur', changed name to Tottenham Hotspur in 1885. Former Grounds: Tottenham Marshes and Northumberland Park, moved to White Hart Lane in 1899. F.A. Cup winner 1901 (as a non-League club). Record attendance 75,038.
(Total) Current Capacity: 36,257 (all seated)
Visiting Supporters' Allocation: 3,000 (in South and West Stands)
Club Colours: White shirts, navy blue shorts
Nearest Railway Station: White Hart Lane plus Seven Sisters and Manor House (tube)

Parking (Car): Street parking (min ¼ mile from ground)
Parking (Coach/Bus): Northumberland Park coach park
Police Force and Tel No: Metropolitan (0208 801 3443)
Disabled Visitors' Facilities:
Wheelchairs: North and South Stands (by prior arrangement)
Blind: Commentary available
Anticipated Development(s): The local council gave permission in October 2001 for the construction of a third tier on the East Stand taking capacity to 44,000, although there is no schedule for the work and it depends on other local regeneration work. Despite the potential that this increase offers, the club is still interested ultimately in relocation.

KEY

C Club Offices
S Club Shop
E Entrance(s) for visiting supporters
R Refreshment bars for visiting supporters
T Toilets for visiting supporters

⬆ North direction (approx)

❶ Park Lane
❷ A1010 High Road
❸ White Hart Lane BR station
❹ Paxton Road
❺ Worcester Avenue
❻ West Stand
❼ South Stand

Above: 695627; *Right:* 695621

It must have been something about the number 13. As the club marked the death of legend Bill Nicholson in early November, the 13th manager to hold the job since Nicholson's departure — Jacques Santini — resigned after a reign of 13 games and with the club on 13 points. Whilst the team had started reasonably well under his command, results in October were poor. The club moved quickly, appointing Martin Jol, an associate of the club's then Director of Football Frank Arnesen, from within the club. Under Jol the club made steady progress, although hopes for a place in the UEFA Cup were not to be fulfilled as a late drop in form resulted in the club finishing in ninth place. Last minute hopes that the club would gain entry to the UEFA Cup through the fair-play places were also dashed. After the season ended, the club was involved in controversy with accusations that Chelsea had made illicit advances to Arnesen to move to Stamford Bridge; the implication of this are unclear at the time of writing but Jol has been strengthening his squad and the expectation at White Hart Lane will be a final place in 2005/06 bringing automatic entry into the UEFA Cup.

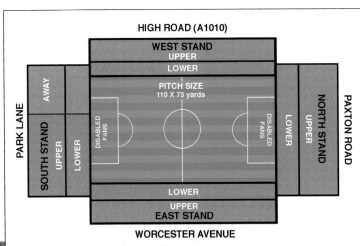

HIGH ROAD (A1010)

WEST STAND
UPPER
LOWER

PITCH SIZE
110 X 73 yards

PARK LANE

SOUTH STAND — AWAY — UPPER — LOWER

DISABLED FANS

DISABLED FANS

LOWER — UPPER — NORTH STAND

PAXTON ROAD

LOWER
UPPER
EAST STAND

WORCESTER AVENUE

TRANMERE ROVERS

Prenton Park, Prenton Road West, Birkenhead, CH42 9PY

Tel No: 0870 460 3333
Advance Tickets Tel No: 0870 460 3332
Fax: 0151 609 0606
Web Site: www.tranmererovers.premiumtv.co.uk
E-Mail: info@tranmererovers.co.uk
League: League One
Brief History: Founded 1884 as Belmont F.C., changed name to Tranmere Rovers in 1885 (not connected to earlier 'Tranmere Rovers'). Former grounds: Steele's Field and Ravenshaw's Field (also known as Old Prenton Park, ground of Tranmere Rugby Club), moved to (new) Prenton Park in 1911. Founder-members 3rd Division North (1921).

Record attendance 24,424
(Total) Current Capacity: 16,587 (all seated)
Visiting Supporters' Allocation: 2,500 (all-seated) in Cow Shed Stand
Club Colours: White shirts, white shorts
Nearest Railway Station: Hamilton Square or Rock Ferry
Parking (Car): Car park at Ground
Parking (Coach/Bus): Car park at Ground
Police Force and Tel No: Merseyside (0151 709 6010)
Disabled Visitors' Facilities:
  Wheelchairs: Main Stand
  Blind: Commentary available

KEY

C Club Offices
S Club Shop
E Entrance(s) for visiting supporters

↑ North direction (approx)

❶ Car Park
❷ Prenton Road West
❸ Borough Road
❹ M53 Junction 4 (B5151) – 3 miles
❺ Birkenhead (1 mile)
❻ Cow Shed Stand
❼ Kop Shed

Above: 698977; *Right:* 698983

Taking over at Prenton Park during the 2003/04 season, Brian Little's experience ensured a reasonable finish to that campaign and ensured that Rovers were one of the pre-season favourites to make progress in League One towards the Play-Offs or automatic promotion. With Hull and Luton dominating the division, Tranmere didn't disappoint as far as reaching the Play-offs were concerned, finishing in third place, seven points adrift of promoted Hull. In the Play-Off semi-final Rovers faced Hartlepool United; losing 2-0 at the Victoria Ground in the first leg, a 2-0 victory at Prenton Park after extra time ensured that the tie went to penalties. Unfortunately for Rovers, Hartlepool's players proved more effective at taking spot kicks with the result that League One fare will again be on offer at Prenton Park in 2005/06. Rovers will, however, be again one of the favourites for promotion and should again feature in the chase for automatic promotion.

BOROUGH ROAD

BOROUGH ROAD (JOHN KING) STAND

PITCH SIZE
110 X 70 yards

PRENTON ROAD WEST

COW SHED STAND
AWAY

KOP STAND

DISABLED FANS

MAIN STAND

P (PERMIT HOLDERS ONLY)

WALSALL

Bescot Stadium, Bescot Crescent, Walsall, West Midlands, WS1 4SA

Tel No: 0870 442 0442
Advance Tickets Tel No: 0870 442 0111
Fax: 01922 613202
Web Site: www.saddlers.premiumtv.co.uk/
E-Mail: info@walsallfc.co.uk
League: League One
Brief History: Founded 1888 as Walsall Town Swifts (amalgamation of Walsall Town – founded 1884 – and Walsall Swifts – founded 1885), changed name to Walsall in 1895. Former Grounds: The Chuckery, West Bromwich Road (twice), Hilary Street (later named Fellows Park, twice), moved to Bescot Stadium in 1990. Founder-members Second Division (1892). Record attendance 10,628 (25,343 at Fellows Park)
(Total) Current Capacity: 11,300 (all seated) (prior to redevelopment)
Visiting Supporters' Allocation: 2,000 maximum in William Sharp Stand

Club Colours: Red shirts, red shorts
Nearest Railway Station: Bescot
Parking (Car): Car park at Ground
Parking (Coach/Bus): Car park at Ground
Police Force and Tel No: West Midlands (01922 638111)
Disabled Visitors' Facilities:
  Wheelchairs: Bank's Stand
  Blind: No special facility
Anticipated Development(s): Planning permission was granted in the summer of 2004 for the redevelopment of the William Sharp Stand to add a further 2,300 seats, taking the away allocation up to 4,000 and the total ground capacity to 13,500. The project is to be funded via advertising directed towards the adjacent M6 and, provided that funding is in place, work is expected to have started in the summer of 2005.

KEY

C Club Offices
S Club Shop
E Entrance(s) for visiting supporters

↑ North direction (approx)

❶ Motorway M6
❷ M6 Junction 9
❸ Bescot BR Station
❹ Car Parks
❺ Bescot Crescent
❻ Gilbert Alsop Stand
❼ William Sharp Stand

Above: 695539; *Right:* 695531

Relegated at the end of 2003/04, much was expected of Paul Merson's Walsall team in League One. However, the optimism was misplaced and, for a period, it looked as though the Saddlers were going to drawn into the League One relegation struggle. And it wasn't only in the League that the team failed to perform: the first round of the FA Cup witnessed defeat away at non-league Slough by 2-1. In the event, the team picked up enough points to ensure that the team finished in 14th position, equidistant between the drop zone and the Play-Offs. Form in the latter part of the season suggests that Walsall could be one of the teams to challenge for a Play-Off position in 2005/06.

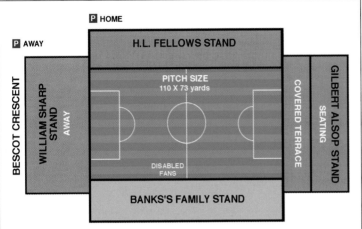

WATFORD

Vicarage Road Stadium, Vicarage Road, Watford, WD18 0ER

Tel No: 01923 496000
Advance Tickets Tel No: 0870 111 1881
Fax: 01923 496001
Web Site: www.watfordfc.premiumtv.co.uk
E-Mail: yourvoice@watfordfc.com
League: League Championship
Brief History: Founded 1898 as an amalgamation of West Herts (founded 1891) and Watford St. Mary's (founded early 1890s). Former Grounds: Wiggenhall Road (Watford St. Mary's) and West Herts Sports Ground, moved to Vicarage Road in 1922. Founder-members Third Division (1920). Record attendance 34,099
(Total) Current Capacity: 20,250 (all seated)
Visiting Supporters' Allocation: 4,500 maximum in Vicarage Road (North) Stand
Club Colours: Yellow shirts, red shorts
Nearest Railway Station: Watford High Street or Watford Junction
Parking (Car): Nearby multi-storey car park in town centre (10 mins walk)

Parking (Coach/Bus): Cardiff Road car park
Other Clubs Sharing Ground: Saracens RUFC
Police Force and Tel No: Hertfordshire (01923 472000)
Disabled Visitors' Facilities:
    Wheelchairs: Corner East Stand and South Stand (special enclosure for approx. 24 wheelchairs), plus enclosure in North East Corner
    Blind: Commentary available in the East Stand (20 seats, free of charge)
Anticipated Development(s): The club's plans for the reconstruction of the East Stand are still in abeyance. However, as a result of safety concerns, part of the existing structure was closed during the close season of 2004, reducing the ground's capacity. This necessitated relocating some 600 season ticket holders as well as the board and press box. The plans for the new stand, for which there remains no definite timescale, anticipate the construction of a new 4,500-seat structure, taking Watford's capacity to 23,000.

KEY
C Club Offices
S Club Shop

↑ North direction (approx)

❶ Vicarage Road
❷ Occupation Road
❸ Rous Stand
❹ Town Centre (¹/₂ mile) – Car Parks, High Street BR Station
❺ Vicarage Road Stand (away)
❻ East Stand
❼ Rookery End

Above: 695969; Right: 695965

Despite guiding the Hornets to a Carling Cup semi-final, where the team lost over two legs to Liverpool, disappointing league form in early 2005, with only four wins in 24 matches resulting in the team dropping towards the relegation zone, saw Ray Lewington sacked as manager in late March. The club moved quickly to appoint his successor, with Adrian Boothroyd arriving on a 12-month rolling contract. Under Boothroyd the club's League Championship position was secured — a 1-0 victory in the penultimate game of the season being sufficient to guarantee the team's status — but defeat in the final game of the season, against West Ham, meant that the club finished in 18th position only two points above relegated Gillingham. During the close season Watford will probably struggle to retain some of its leading players, such as Heidar Helguson, and how the club performs in 2005/06 will depend greatly on the quality of the players that Boothroyd manages to attract. The suspicion is that it could be another season of struggle at Vicarage Road.

WEST BROMWICH ALBION

The Hawthorns, Halfords Lane, West Bromwich, West Midlands, B71 4LF

Tel No: 08700 668888
Advance Tickets Tel No: 08700 662800
Fax: 08700 662861
Web Site: www.wba.premiumtv.co.uk
E-Mail: enquiries@wbafc.co.uk
League: F.A. Premier
Brief History: Founded 1879. Former
Grounds: Coopers Hill, Dartmouth Park, Four
Acres, Stoney Lane, moved to the Hawthorns
in 1900. Founder-members of Football League
(1888). Record attendance 64,815
(Total) Current Capacity: 28,000 (all seated)
Visiting Supporters' Allocation: 3,000 in
Smethwick End (can be increased to 5,200 if
required)
Club Colours: Navy blue and white striped
shirts, white shorts

Nearest Railway Station: The Hawthorns
Parking (Car): Halfords Lane and Rainbow
Stand car parks
Parking (Coach/Bus): Rainbow Stand car park
Police Force and Tel No: West Midlands (0121
554 3414)
Disabled Visitors' Facilities:
  Wheelchairs: Apollo 2000 and Smethwick
  Road End
  Blind: Facility available
Anticipated Development(s): There is
speculation that the club will seek to increase
capacity to 30,000 by rebuilding the area
between the Apollo and East stands, but
nothing is confirmed.

KEY

C Club Offices
S Club Shop
E Entrance(s) for visiting
   supporters

⬆ North direction (approx)

❶ A41 Birmingham Road
❷ To M5 Junction 1
❸ Birmingham Centre (4 miles)
❹ Halfords Lane
❺ Main Stand
❻ Smethwick End
❼ Rolfe Street, Smethwick BR
   Station (1½ miles)
❽ To The Hawthorns BR
   Station
❾ East (Rainbow) Stand
❿ Apollo 2000 Stand

Above: 699262; Right: 699266

With the Baggies struggling towards the wrong end of the table, with eight points from 10 games and after a 3-0 defeat at bottom team Crystal Palace, Gary Megson announced at the end of October that he wouldn't be renewing his contract with the club at the end of the season. When this had occurred elsewhere, most notably at Southampton in 2003/4 with Gordon Strachan, the 'lame-dog' manager failed to see out the season and so it also proved at The Hawthorns with Megson failing to last the day before he was relieved of his duties! Frank Burrows took temporary charges of the team before former Baggies hero (and ex-Middlesbrough and Bradford City manager) Brian Robson was appointed to the post in early November. Not universally welcomed on his arrival, the early results seemed to confirm Robson's critics correct. However, he was able to keep the team close to safety and, in a dramatic finale to the season, the Baggies pulled off one of the great escapes in footballing history. Starting the final day in last place, West Brom needed to defeat Portsmouth at home and hope that none of the three teams above them achieved wins. Victory over Portsmouth meant that West Brom did their part of the bargain and with both Norwich and Southampton losing, everything depended on the result at The Valley, where Charlton were playing host to Crystal Palace. A Charlton equaliser in the dying minutes was enough to see West Brom survive and Palace relegated, thus ensuring Premier League football at the Hawthorns again in 2005/06. However, the squad will need to improve dramatically if it is again to survive and it's hard to escape the conclusion that another battle against the drop beckons in this part of the West Midlands.

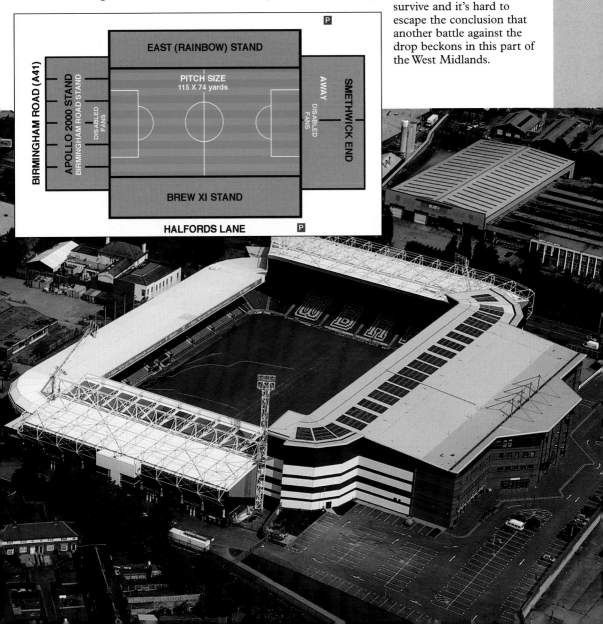

WEST HAM UNITED

Boleyn Ground, Green Street, Upton Park, London, E13 9AZ

Tel No: 020 8548 2748
Advance Tickets Tel No: 0870 112 2700
Fax: 020 8548 2758
Web Site: www.whufc.co.uk
E-Mail: yourcomments@westhamunited.co.uk
League: F.A. Premier
Brief History: Founded 1895 as Thames Ironworks, changed name to West Ham United in 1900. Former Grounds: Hermit Road, Browning Road, The Memorial Ground, moved to Boleyn Ground in 1904. Record attendance 42,322
(Total) Current Capacity: 35,647 (all seated)
Visiting Supporters' Allocation: 3,700 maximum
Club Colours: Claret and blue shirts, white shorts
Nearest Railway Station: Barking BR, Upton Park (tube)
Parking (Car): Street parking
Parking (Coach/Bus): As directed by Police

Police Force and Tel No: Metropolitan (020 8593 8232)
Disabled Visitors' Facilities:
  Wheelchairs: West Lower, Bobby Moore and Centenary Stands
  Blind: Commentaries available
Anticipated Development(s): The new 15,247-seat Dr Martens Stand opened in November 2001. The next phase of the ground's redevelopment will see the reconstruction of the East Stand. Although the club had plans to reconstruct the East Stand and extend both the Bobby Moore and Centenary stands, with a view to increasing the ground's capacity to 40,000, this work had been deferred as a result of relegation and the loss of income that playing in the League Championship resulted in.

KEY

E Entrance(s) for visiting supporters

↑ North direction (approx)

❶ A124 Barking Road
❷ Green Street
❸ North Stand
❹ Upton Park Tube Station (1/4 mile)
❺ Barking BR Station (1 mile)
❻ Bobby Moore Stand
❼ East Stand
❽ West Stand

Above: 699352; Right: 699342

A difficult season for West Ham with fans frustrated at the team's inability to make a serious challenge for promotion ultimately saw the team grab a Play-Off position courtesy of results on the last day of the season. The Hammers' victory away at Watford combined with Reading's defeat at Wigan was enough to ensure West Ham's presence in the Play-Offs. In the Semi-Finals the club faced Ipswich and, after a 2-2 draw at Upton Park, it appeared as though the Suffolk side was in the driving seat. However, in the return match, West Ham were victorious 2-0, thus setting up a final against Preston North End at the Millennium Stadium. For much of the season Alan Pardew's position seemed to be under threat and this was confirmed by comments made by players after the final at the Millennium Stadium. In the event, the Hammers' 1-0 victory of Preston North End guaranteed a return to the Premier League for the east London tram after two seasons in the Championship. However, it's hard to escape the conclusion that, like other promoted teams, West Ham will struggle to survive, particularly as the club is still hidebound by multi-million pound of debt. Given the background, West Ham will in all probability feature in the battle to avoid the drop and consolidation, and 17th place, is perhaps the best that fans can look forward to.

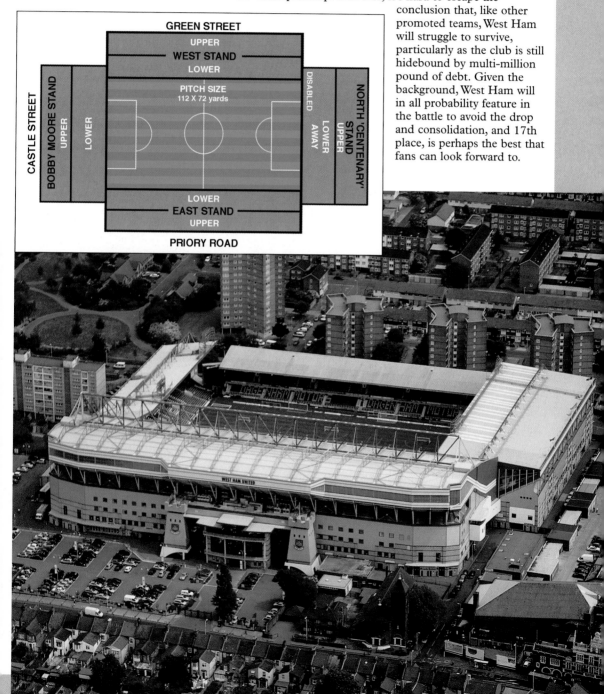

GREEN STREET

UPPER

WEST STAND

LOWER

PITCH SIZE
112 X 72 yards

CASTLE STREET

BOBBY MOORE STAND

UPPER

LOWER

DISABLED

NORTH 'CENTENARY' STAND

LOWER AWAY

UPPER

LOWER

EAST STAND

UPPER

PRIORY ROAD

WEST HAM UNITED

WIGAN ATHLETIC

JJB Stadium, Robin Park Complex, Newtown, Wigan, Lancashire WN5 0UZ

Tel No: 01942 774000
Advance Tickets Tel No: 0870 112 2552
Fax: 01942 770477
Web Site: www.wiganlatics.premiumtv.co.uk
E-Mail: s.hayton@jjbstadium.co.uk
League: F.A. Premier
Brief History: Founded 1932. Springfield Park used by former Wigan Borough (Football League 1921-1931) but unrelated to current club. Elected to Football League in 1978 (the last club to be elected rather than promoted). Moved to JJB Stadium for start of 1999/2000 season. Record attendance at Springfield Park 27,500; at JJB Stadium 20,669
(Total) Current Capacity: 25,000 (all-seated)
Visiting Supporters' Allocation: 8,178 (maximum) in East (Adidas) Stand (all-seated)

Club Colours: White and blue shirts, blue shorts
Nearest Railway Stations: Wigan Wallgate/Wigan North Western (both about 1.5 miles away)
Parking (Car): 2,500 spaces at the ground
Parking (Coach/Bus): As directed
Other Clubs Sharing Ground: Wigan Warriors RLFC
Police Force and Tel No: Greater Manchester (0161 872 5050)
Disabled Visitors' Facilities
   Wheelchairs: 100 spaces
   Blind: No special facility although it is hoped to have a system in place shortly
Anticipated Development(s): None following completion of the ground.

KEY

C Club Offices
E Entrance(s) for visiting supporters

↑ North direction (approx)

❶ Loire Drive
❷ Anjoy Boulevard
❸ Car Parks
❹ Robin Park Arena
❺ River Douglas
❻ Leeds-Liverpool Canal
❼ To A577/A49 and Wigan town centre plus Wigan (Wallgate) and Wigan (North Western) station
❽ East Stand
❾ South Stand
❿ North Stand
⓫ West Stand

Above: 699269; Right: 699272

Having just missed out on the Play-Offs in the most cruel way at the end of 2003/04, many wondered whether Athletic could get over their disappointment and again mount a serious challenge for promotion. In the event, Paul Jewell's team were in the automatic promotion places for much of the season, vying with both Sunderland and Ipswich for the top two spots. In the event, Sunderland strode off with the title and it came down to last day nerves — again — as Wigan faced Reading at home and Ipswich played Brighton away. Victory 3-1 at home ensured Wigan's promotion, bringing top flight football to the town for the first time. Inevitably, Wigan will be installed as one of the pre-season favourites for an immediate return to the Championship, but in Dave Whelan the club has a chairman willing and able to dig deep in his pockets and in Paul Jewell a manager who has experienced bringing an unfashionable team, Bradford City, in to the Premier League and in ensuring its survival for a season against the odds. Whilst Athletic will undoubtedly struggle, it won't be a complete surprise if, come May 2006, the team is 17th.

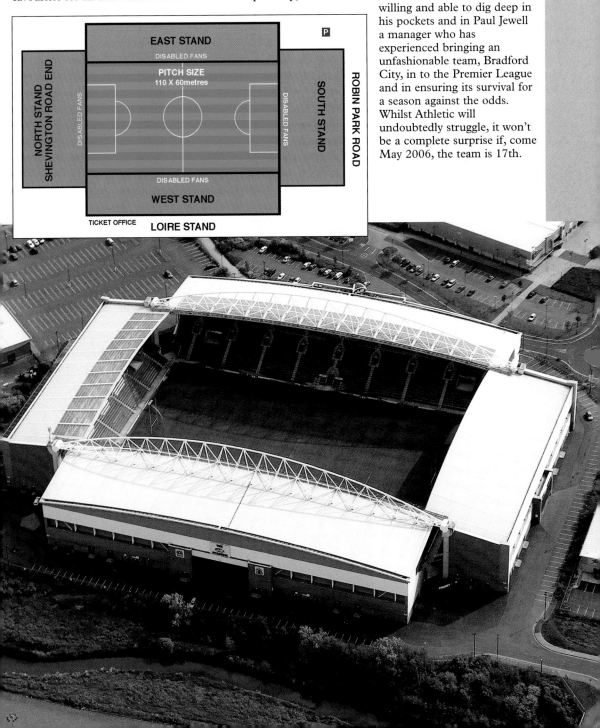

WOLVERHAMPTON WANDERERS

Molineux Ground, Waterloo Road, Wolverhampton, WV1 4QR

Tel No: 0870 442 0123
Advance Tickets Tel No: 0870 442 0123
Fax: 01902 687006
Web Site: www.wolves.premiumtv.co.uk
E-Mail: info@wolves.co.uk
League: League Championship
Brief History: Founded 1877 as St. Lukes, combined with Goldthorn Hill to become Wolverhampton Wanderers in 1884. Former Grounds: Old Windmill Field, John Harper's Field and Dudley Road, moved to Molineux in 1889. Founder-members Football League (1888). Record attendance 61,315
(Total) Current Capacity: 29,400 (all seated)
Visiting Supporters' Allocation: 3,200 in lower tier of Steve Bull Stand or 2,000 in Jack Harris Stand
Club Colours: Gold shirts, black shorts
Nearest Railway Station: Wolverhampton

Parking (Car): West Park and adjacent North Bank
Parking (Coach/Bus): As directed by Police
Police Force and Tel No: West Midlands (01902 649000)
Disabled Visitors' Facilities:
Wheelchairs: 104 places on two sides
Blind: Commentary (by prior arrangement)
Anticipated Developments: The club installed some 900 seats on a temporary stand between the Billy Wright and Jack Harris stands for the season in the Premiership. The club has plans to expand the capacity of Molineux to more than 40,000 by adding second tiers to the Stan Cullis and Jack Harris stands and completely rebuilding the Steve Bull Stand. There is no timescale for the work but it is unlikely to proceed until the club regains (and retains) a place in the Premiership.

KEY
C Club Offices
S Club Shop
E Entrance(s) for visiting supporters
R Refreshment bars for visiting supporters
T Toilets for visiting supporters

↑ North direction (approx)

❶ Stan Cullis Stand
❷ Steve Bull Stand
❸ Billy Wright Stand
❹ Ring Road – St. Peters
❺ Waterloo Road
❻ A449 Stafford Street
❼ BR Station (¹/₂ mile)
❽ Jack Harris Stand
❾ Molineux Street
❿ Molineux Way
⓫ Temporary additional seating

Above: 696908; Right: 696013

Following a very disappointing start to the season, culminating in a 1-0 defeat away at Gillingham that left Wolves just above the League Championship drop zone, Dave Jones was sacked as manager at the start of November. Stuart Gray took over as caretaker with the media speculating widely over a range of possible full-time appointments. In the event, the club appointed ex-England and Spurs boss Glenn Hoddle to take over initially with a six-month contract. Under Hoddle, Wolves' form improved considerably and, if the season had been a bit longer, the club might have sneaked into the Play-offs. As it was, finishing in ninth place, seven points adrift of sixth-placed West Ham, was far better than Wolves' fans might have anticipated when Hoddle took over. With Hoddle now confirmed as manager for 2005/06, the foundations have been laid for a potentially successful campaign and Wolves should certainly be one of the challengers for automatic promotion.

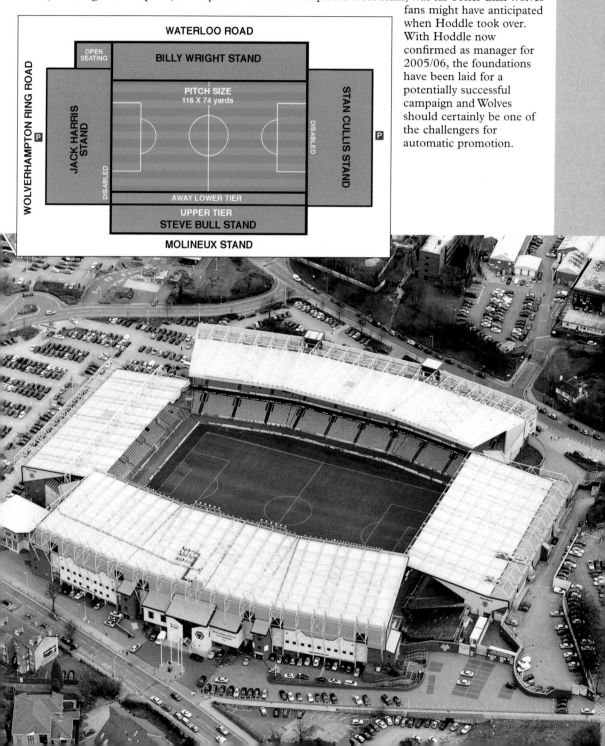

WREXHAM

Racecourse Ground, Mold Road, Wrexham, Clwyd LL11 2AH

Tel No: 01978 262129
Advance Tickets Tel No: 01978 366388
Web Site: www.wrexhamafc.premiumtv.co.uk
E-Mail: geraint@wrexhamfc.co.uk
Fax: 01978 357821
League: League Two
Brief History: Founded 1873 (oldest Football Club in Wales). Former Ground: Acton Park, permanent move to Racecourse Ground c.1900. Founder-members Third Division North (1921). Record attendance 34,445
(Total) Current Capacity: 15,500 (11,500 seated)
Visiting Supporters' Allocation: 3,100 (maximum; all seated)
Club Colours: Red shirts, white shorts
Nearest Railway Station: Wrexham General
Parking (Car): (Nearby) Town car parks
Parking (Coach/Bus): As directed by Police
Police Force and Tel No: Wrexham Division (01978 290222)
Disabled Visitors' Facilities:

Wheelchairs: Pryce Griffiths Stand
Blind: No special facility
Anticipated Development(s): The club's then new managing director announced after the end of the 2003/04 season that the club was investigating the possibility of redevelopment at the Racecourse Ground in order to maximise the potential from the site. This work would include rebuilding the ground following rotation of the pitch by 90°. However, the position has become highly complicated with the club entering Administration and with the freehold of the ground being owned by Alex Hamilton. There are a number of possible bidders to take the club over, including one that intends to proceed with the partial redevelopment of the ground whilst still allowing Wrexham to play there. At the time of writing, nothing is confirmed with regards to the future of the Racecourse Ground although the assumption is that the club will continue to play there during the 2005/06 season.

KEY

C Club Offices
S Club Shop
E Entrance(s) for visiting supporters
R Refreshment bars for visiting supporters
T Toilets for visiting supporters

↑ North direction (approx)

❶ Wrexham General Station
❷ A541 – Mold Road
❸ Wrexham Town Centre
❹ Pryce Griffiths Stand
❺ Kop Town End
❻ To Wrexham Central Station
❼ Roberts Builders Stand (away)

Above: 685071; *Right:* 685072

A disastrous season for Wrexham both one and off the field left supporters wondering whether they'd have a team to support in 2005/06 and, if they did, where it would be playing. The club collapsed into Administration during the season and therefore became the first team to be penalised by the deduction of 10 points for so doing. This dragged the team into the relegation zone from where it was unable to escape, resulting in League Two football in the new season. On the field, Denis Smith's team would have escaped the drop — just — if the points hadn't been deducted and Milton Keynes would have been relegated in their place. There was one high point, however, victory over Southend United in the LDV trophy at the Millennium Stadium, although fans would probably have sacrificed this result for stability both on and off the pitch. Given the problems off the field, in particular the threat to redevelop the Racecourse Ground, it's hard to be optimistic about the new season as players will drift away from the club in the close season unless its future is rapidly ensured. However, as Bradford City showed in the summer of 2004 it is possible to come out of Administration, acquire effectively a new squad and still make positive progress on the field.

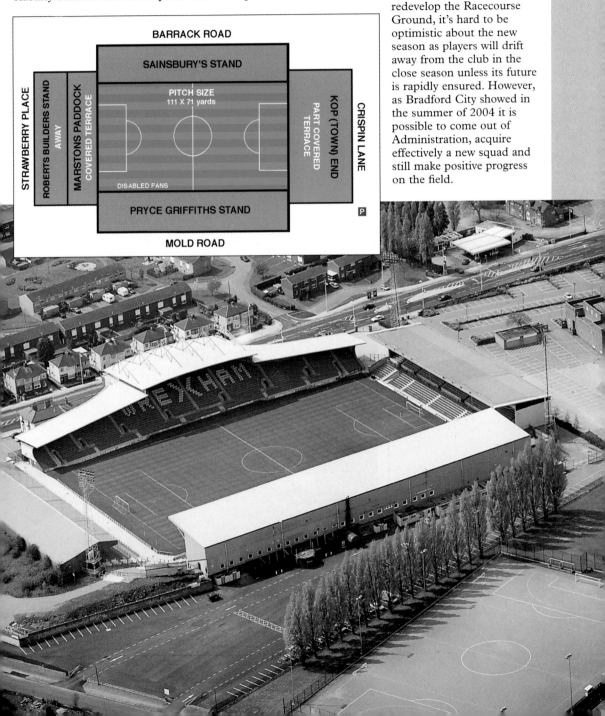

BARRACK ROAD

SAINSBURY'S STAND

PITCH SIZE
111 X 71 yards

STRAWBERRY PLACE

ROBERTS BUILDERS STAND
AWAY

MARSTONS PADDOCK
COVERED TERRACE

PART COVERED
TERRACE

KOP (TOWN) END

CRISPIN LANE

DISABLED FANS

PRYCE GRIFFITHS STAND

P

MOLD ROAD

WYCOMBE WANDERERS

Causeway Stadium, Hillbottom Road, Sands, High Wycombe, Bucks HP12 4HJ

Tel No: 01494 472100
Advance Tickets Tel No: 01494 441118
Fax: 01494 527633
Web Site: www.wycombewanderers.premiumtv.co.uk
E-Mail: wwfc@wycombewanderers.co.uk
League: League Two
Brief History: Founded 1884. Former Grounds: The Rye, Spring Meadows, Loakes Park, moved to Adams Park 1990. Promoted to Football League 1993. Record attendance 15,678 (Loakes Park); 9,921 (Adams Park)
(Total) Current Capacity: 10,000 (8,250 seated)
Visiting Supporters' Allocation: c2,000 in the Roger Vere Stand
Club Colours: Sky blue with navy blue quartered shirts, blue shorts
Nearest Railway Station: High Wycombe (2½ miles)

Parking (Car): At Ground and Street parking
Parking (Coach/Bus): At Ground
Other Clubs Sharing Ground: London Wasps RUFC
Police Force and Tel No: Thames Valley (01494 465888)
Disabled Visitors' Facilities:
  Wheelchairs: Special shelter – Main Stand, Hillbottom Road end
  Blind: Commentary available
Anticipated Development(s): The club has tentative plans to increase the ground's capacity to some 12-15,000 through the redevelopment of the Main Stand. There is, however, no timescale for this work, a project that would also require the construction of a new access road.

KEY

C Club Offices
S Club Shop
E Entrance(s) for visiting supporters

↑ North direction (approx)

❶ Car Park
❷ Hillbottom Road (Industrial Estate)
❸ M40 Junction 4 (approx 2 miles)
❹ Wycombe Town Centre (approx 2½ miles)
❺ Woodlands Stand
❻ Roger Vere Stand (away)
❼ Syan Stand
❽ Amersham & Wycombe College Stand

Above: 699217; Right: 699226

After a year as manager, Tony Adams announced his resignation in early November 'for personal reasons'. Although he had failed to keep the team up the previous season, the 2004/05 campaign had started well with the team top of the division in early September. Results since then were poor, with the team taking just four points from eight games to plummet down the table. The assistant manager oversaw the cup victory at Coalville but then he too left the club with Keith Ryan being appointed caretaker player-manager. At the end of November, John Gorman was appointed new full-time manager. Bringing in some experienced players, such as Rob Lee, stabilised the Wycombe ship and, ultimately, the club finished in 10th position, missing out on the Play-Offs by some seven points. If the late season form can be maintained into the new season, then there is every possibility that Gorman can push the club towards either promotion or the Play-Offs.

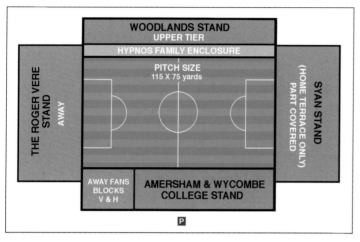

WOODLANDS STAND
UPPER TIER
HYPNOS FAMILY ENCLOSURE
PITCH SIZE
115 X 75 yards

THE ROGER VERE STAND
AWAY

SYAN STAND
(HOME TERRACE ONLY)
PART COVERED

AWAY FANS BLOCKS V & H

AMERSHAM & WYCOMBE COLLEGE STAND

P

YEOVIL TOWN

Huish Park, Lufton Way, Yeovil, Somerset BA22 8YF

Tel No: 01935 423662
Advance Tickets Tel No: 01935 423662
Fax: 01935 473956
Web Site: www.ytfc.premiumtv.co.uk
E-Mail: media@ytfc.net
League League One
Brief History: Founded as Yeovil Casuals in 1895 and merged with Petters United in 1920. Moved to old ground (Huish) in 1920 and relocated to Huish Park in 1990. Founder members of Alliance Premier League in 1979 but relegated in 1985. Returned to Premier League in 1988 but again relegated in 1996. Promoted to the now retitled Conference in 1997 and promoted to the Nationwide League in 2003. Record Attendance: (at Huish) 16,318 (at Huish Park) 9,348

(Total) Current Capacity: 9,400 (5,212 seated)
Visiting Supporters' Allocation: 1,700 on Copse Road Terrace (open) plus c400 seats in Bartlett Stand.
Club Colours: Green shirts, white shorts
Nearest Railway Station: Yeovil Junction or Yeovil Pen Mill
Parking (Car): Car park near to stadium for 800 cars
Parking (Coach/Bus): As directed
Police Force and Tel No: Avon & Somerset (01935 415291)
Disabled Visitors' Facilities:
　Wheelchairs: Up to 20 dedicated located in the Bartlett Stand
　Blind: No special facility

KEY

🡑　North direction (approx)

❶　Western Avenue
❷　Copse Road
❸　Lufton Way
❹　Artillery Road
❺　Main (Yeovil College) Stand
❻　Bartlett Stand
❼　Westland Stand
❽　Copse Road Terrace (away)
❾　Memorial Road
❿　Mead Avenue
⓫　To town centre (one mile) and stations (two to four miles)

190　　　*Above:* 695579; *Right:* 695573

Town's second season in the League was to be one of considerable success for Gary Johnson's team as the side achieved both promotion and the League Two title. However, it was a close run thing with any one of four teams potentially failing to make the top three come the final Saturday of the season. In the event, Yeovil's 3-0 home victory over Lincoln, combined with the results for Swansea, Scunthorpe and Southend confirmed Yeovil as champions and condemned the Essex team to the Play-Offs. Elsewhere, there was success in both the Carling Cup — where the team defeated Plymouth (then second in the League Championship) — and in the Third Round of the FA Cup — over Rotherham at Millmoor (perhaps given the Millers' form this was, however, no surprise) — to show that the club's League status hadn't altered its tradition of giantkilling. With promotion to League One, Yeovil can renew acquaintance not only with Rotherham but also with Doncaster, who were promoted from the Conference in the same year that Yeovil made the leap. Doncaster's example shows that it is possible for a team from League Two to prosper at this higher level and Yeovil has the potential to achieve this.

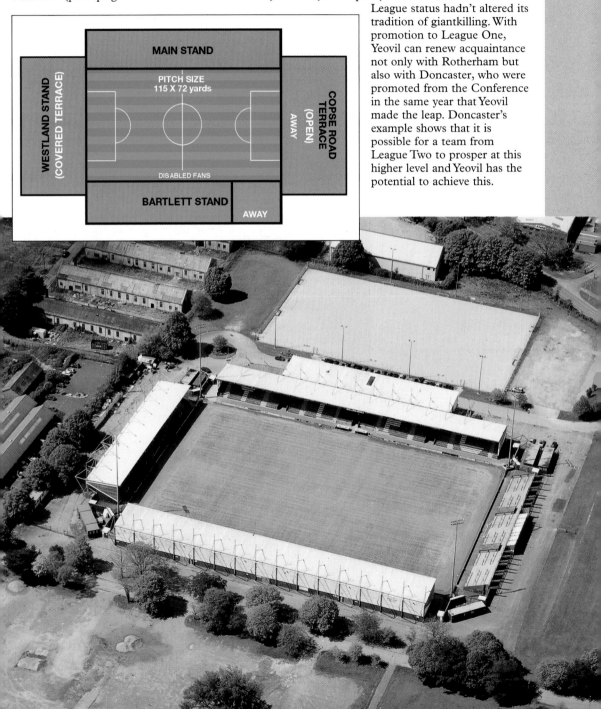

WEMBLEY

Wembley Stadium, Wembley HA9 0DW

Tel No: tbc
Advance Tickets Tel No: tbc
Fax: tbc
Brief History: Inaugurated for FA Cup Final of 1923, venue for many major national and international matches including the World Cup Final of 1966. Also traditionally used for other major sporting events and as a venue for rock concerts and other entertainments. Last used prior to redevelopment as a football ground versus Germany in October 2001. Ground subsequently demolished during late 2002.
(Total) Current Capacity: tbc
Nearest Railway Station: Wembley Complex (National Rail), Wembley Central (National Rail and London Underground), Wembley Park (London Underground)

Parking (Car): Limited parking at ground and nearby
Parking (Coach Bus): As advised by police
Police Force: Metropolitan
Disabled Facilities
  Wheelchairs: tbc
  Blind: tbc
Anticipated Development(s): After several years of dithering and following the final game played at the 'old' Wembley, demolition of the old ground was completed in late 2002 and work started on the construction of the new stadium. This is scheduled for completion in 2006 and it is hoped that the completed ground will host the 2006 FA Cup Final.

Above: 699006